The LMS in the WEST MIDLANDS

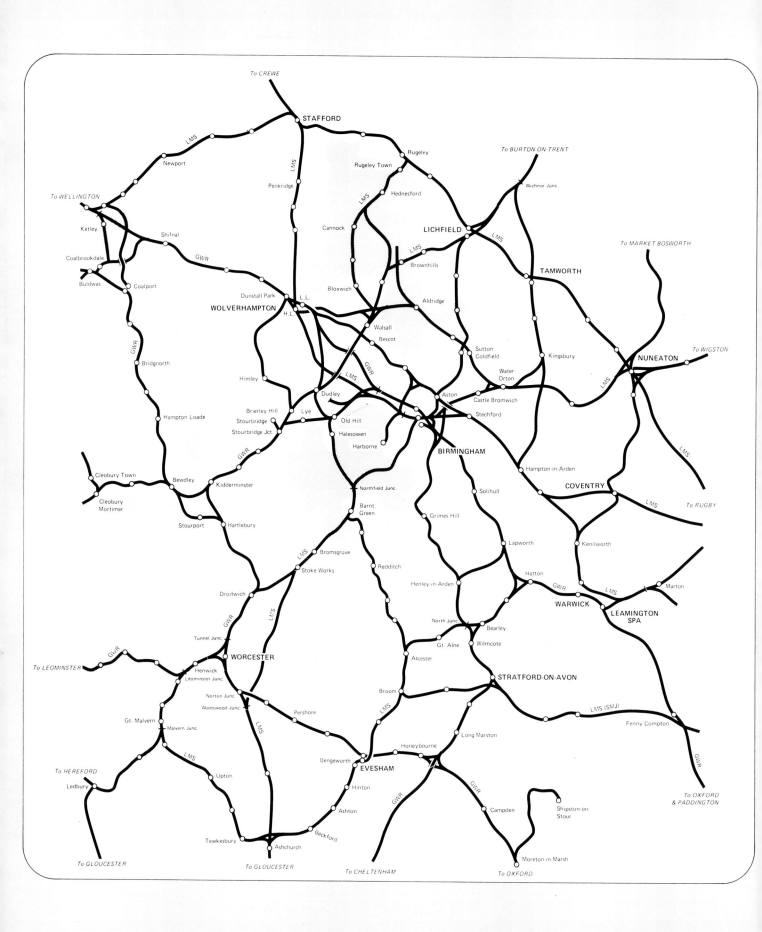

The
LMS
in the
WEST MIDLANDS

P. B. Whitehouse

Oxford Publishing Company

Typesetting by:
MS Filmsetting Limited, Frome, Somerset
Printed in Great Britain by:
Balding + Mansell Ltd, Wisbech, Cambs

Published by:
Oxford Publishing Co.
Link House
West Street
Poole, Dorset

Bibliography

I have consulted the following books to try to obtain information regarding dates, locomotive names, numbers and shed workings, aswell as some historical background. All are commended to those who wish to obtain knowledge of the LMS in the West Midlands.

Railways of the West Midlands 1808–1954		Stephenson Locomotive Society
Locomotives at the Grouping LMS	H. C. Casserley	Ian Allan Ltd
ABC British Railways Locomotives 1948		Ian Allan Ltd
LMS Engine Sheds Vol 1 LNWR	Hawkins & Reeve	Wild Swan Publications Ltd
LMS Engine Sheds Vol II Midland	Hawkins & Reeve	Wild Swan Publications Ltd
Leek and Manifold Railway	'Manifold'	J. H. Henstock Ltd
LMS Railway Timetables – various		
Bradshaws Railway Guides – various		
Road and Rails of Birmingham 1900–1939	R. T. Coxon	Ian Allan Ltd
A Regional History of the Railways of Great Britain Vol VII: West Midlands	R. Christiansen	David & Charles Ltd
Railway Clearing House Maps		
Railway Clearing House Junction Diagrams		

Contents

Acknowledgements

I am grateful to many people for help with this book, some of this gratitude going back a long time. My parents were happy to encourage, or certainly not discourage, my early love of railways. LMS railway staff (except the station master at Somerset Road) were patient with a small boy and an inquiring adolescent, and my paternal grandmother did more than she could ever have imagined by giving me her cast off Kodak No. 1A folding camera, in 1936. This succeeded a couple of 5s. Coronet box cameras, which did their stuff with the odd stationary train, but the 1A has nominal shutter speeds up to 1/100th second! Certainly the kindness of railwaymen meant much then, and without it, enthusiasm could have lagged seriously.

My collection of pictures covers some 45 years. It began when I saw an advertisement by one W. Leslie Good of Kings Norton, Birmingham for postcards, which at 3d (1½p) each were a find indeed. Leslie was not an easy man to get to know, but I was fortunate in having his friendship. In the end, he sadly became withdrawn, and if it had not been for W. A. Camwell, Ric Green and a few others, his negatives could have and nearly did perish. I would like to pay special tribute to Leslie Good, suspecting that a number of prints credited to my collection are his, and I thank him for them.

Another great photographer of LMS, and particularly ex-LNWR scenes, is Arthur Flowers, and anything that moved within thirty miles of Coventry rarely escaped his lens. Arthur has been more than helpful, and I am extremely grateful to him. Others, including Arthur Camwell, Roger Carpenter, Jack Flemons, Frank Hemming, P. Hopkins, C. F. H. Oldham and Eric Russell have turned out their collections to seek negatives and prints, and I am very appreciative, not only of the assistance they have given, but also for the time spent in thinking out the possibilities available. Credits are, of course, given where possible, but if anyone finds his name missing my apologies, and I hope he will write and let me know.

Dates of photographs taken long ago are not easy to check absolutely. Where it has been possible, I have made them known, but in general the pictures were taken for the joy of the act rather than a record for posterity, but later we learned better. Locations too are sometimes problematical, especially when great change has taken place since the photograph was taken. Usually the photographer can help, but when he has died this then becomes more difficult. I would particularly like to thank John Edgington for his help in confirming a number of locations – we both hope we are right!

Christine Brook has done the typing, and in getting this correct from my handwriting deserves a personal medal.

P. B. Whitehouse
Birmingham 1984

Chapter One   INTRODUCTION

It is rarely possible to identify one's first contact with railways, but I have a dim recollection of being given egg sandwiches on a train journeying from Birmingham to Colwyn Bay, when I was around three years old. Certainly there are memories of many happy holidays in that area in past years, with vague pictures of big black engines seen through wrought iron railings. In those days, the North Wales coastline would have been solid LNW and, maybe, that is when and where my love for its engines was born.

My first real recollections are of being taken down to two local suburban stations on the west side of Birmingham, both within walking distance of where we lived. The first was Harborne, one of the city's two terminal stations, originally a pre-grouping private railway worked by the London & North Western. The second was Somerset Road, on the Midland's Birmingham West Suburban line. Quite when this was I don't know, except that I remember my mother suggesting that we go and look at the 'new red coaches at Harborne', so I would think it was probably around 1926. I certainly remember seeing oil burners at Somerset Road.

The Harborne line was a gentle, pleasant little branch, 2 miles 39 chains long. It ran from a junction with the main Birmingham to Wolverhampton line, just north-west of Monument Lane, and had three intermediate stations, one of these being a passing loop; gradients were as steep as 1 in 66. From a small boy's point of view, Harborne was exciting, as it had a turntable and a run-round loop which meant that there was always a chance of helping to push the engine round, with a subsequent footplate ride. Once, at least, this was on an L&NWR 2-4-0 Jumbo, but more usually, it was on a Webb 0-6-0 or a tank. This, too, was the usual way to go into New Street to watch the trains on Saturdays or during the school holidays, as it was cheaper than the Corporation bus. The latter charged 1½d each way for a child, whilst the train was only 1½d **return**. The advertised time took about as long as the bus, but the problem was fitting into the main line junction and the stop to collect tickets at Monument Lane, New Street being an open station in those days. But it was a good grounding for railway enthusiasm, because there was time enough to talk to the locomotive crews, to see the signalman and the huge single line staff, to learn of far away places like Walsall and Lichfield and above all to be close to the real smell of a steam engine.

Somerset Road was quite different. This was ex-Midland and the station had a stern station master who didn't take to boys standing around on his platforms. So we had to watch from the lattice footbridge connecting the platforms, though this in itself could be an adventure when actually standing over the trains as they thundered past, as much as Midland type trains ever did! Very few trains stopped at Somerset Road, though I do remember once being taken to New Street behind what I now know was an 0-6-4 tank. 'Down stoppers', those going away from Derby, were protected while they tarried at Somerset Road, by home and distant signals controlled from a small frame on the platform. What good that ever did is open to some discussion. I sometimes think that Somerset Road really started my interest in railway photography, for my sister and I were often deposited there by a young lady who took us out for walks in the afternoon. As nature would have it, she soon became friendly with the porter, and when the station master was still dozing in his house after lunch, she would lend me a box camera and take the odd photograph, whilst she disappeared into the porter's room. Sadly, these pictures have not survived and neither did the young lady, after my mother found out about it all. The station closed in 1930, and that was very much that.

The Midland line to the south-west was, however, still a good place to watch trains. In our part of the world, it ran alongside the Birmingham & Worcester canal where horse-drawn boats plied their way in some numbers, and even standing on the footbridge at Somerset Road, I remember hearing the hidden pounding of the horses hooves on the towpath. There was one particular bridge which was really excellent for watching both kinds of traffic. Bright canal barges, belonging to Fellows Morton & Clayton, and red 4-4-0s plus black 0-6-4 'hole in the wall' tanks provided plenty of interest. Until Stanier's arrival in the mid-1930s, nothing larger than a Compound or Fowler 0-6-0 came over the old Midlands metals.

Another place to watch the Midland line trains was Five Ways Station, the first beyond the series of tunnels. Here the snorty 4-4-0 and 0-6-0 locomotives would come smoking past, heading for the playing fields of the big girls' schools in Edgbaston, and the open space surrounding the University. Above the station platforms, on high level tracks, were the two lines going down through Granville Street, the original terminus of the Birmingham West Suburban line, to the Central goods yard in the heart of Birmingham. This was usually shunted by an ex-Midland Class 1F 0-6-0 tank, which popped in and out of the tunnel as it went about its work. On the 'up' line into New Street, was a water column, much used on summer Saturday excursions whose engines were thirstier than some of the passed cleaners helping out had imagined.

Generally, visits to New Street tended to be to the North-Western side, the only big engines appearing in the Midland station being either 'Claughton' or later 'Royal Scot' class locomotives, on the 'Pines Express' when engines were changed. This and the 'Devonian' were the only two named trains we ever saw. The original Midland station managed to outlast that of the North Western, for the overall roof came off much later, and until well into the 1960s, Class 2 4-4-0 locomotives could be seen as Midland side pilots. When the station came to be demolished and 'improved', vast crates of white crockery, emblazoned with Midland insignia, were found in the refreshment room stores. These were given away by the demolition contractors for a small pourboire.

The North-Western side was full of attractions. Always gloomier and never so smart as the Great Western's Snow Hill, there was somehow an atmosphere of smoky haze together with gas-lit homeliness, until the big roof came off after World War II. In the darkness at the south end of main down platform was a signal box and a milk/fish/parcels bay, serviced by a shunter with a horn and a horse. The GWR had horses too, at Snow Hill. The platform extended into that area, but boys were usually chased off, so it therefore remained unexplored. Platform 3 was very short by the standards of the day, and any particularly lengthy northbound train had to overrun and set back into this bay, controlled by the shunter and his horn. Platform access was by way of a footbridge, which was crowned in the middle by an open signal frame and a large clock, whose face could be seen all over the station. Steps down to the platform were wooden, with short risers making ascent and descent easy. As with so many ex-LNW stations in the Midlands, these risers each had a black and yellow enamelled plate drawing passengers' attention to commercial emporiums in the district. The two stations were divided by the Queen's Drive roadway, which was crossed by this bridge. It was like moving into another world when crossing to the other side, and I doubt if one side ever spoke to the other.

There were subways too, both of which were strictly out of bounds, one for luggage and staff and one direct to the GPO, serviced by silent electrically-operated trolleys hauling noisy clattering steel-wheeled trailers. Sometimes we penetrated the former, which was lined with white glazed bricks, but we never summoned up enough courage to delve into the Post Office depths.

New Street, like most other large stations in those days, had train indicators as the sole means of letting the public know which platform their train was to use. Unlike those at Snow Hill, these actually had clock faces at the pinnacles of their posts to tell the times of departure, with the clock fingers being pushed into place by porters, when they remembered. Also there were roller blinds listing train destinations and departure times. All express trains were met on the North-Western side by men in red uniforms who were pages and porters from the Queen's Hotel (telegrams Bestotel) whose lifts descended from the foyer to platform 1, close to the Wymans bookstall.

As we grew older, so New Street changed with us. In the early years, engines appeared in black or red, or various combinations of the two when odd tenders became attached, with cast cabside numerals from Crewe, and huge tender ones thereafter. Coaches were plum and spilt milk and red, headed by engines which made very individual noises as they came in and out. The Midland engines, especially the Class 2 and 3 4-4-0s, would rumble and 'woof' as they went out, but the North-Western's were much more distinctive. These divided themselves into two, firstly the Webb engines, which went 'tink tink, tink tink' as they came in, and 'chaff chaff CHAFF chaff' as they left and the bigger Precursors, George the Fifths and particularly Princes, which really let go with throaty roars slightly off beat (one-two THREE-four) as they made for the 1 in 77 through the dark murky Monument Lane tunnel.

Then came one of the new 'Royal Scots' class locomotives on display. There were steps provided for people to climb into the cab, and her smokebox door was open with the inside painted white. It was the signal for slow but very sure change. In the beginning, outside cylinder engines were rarely seen, but now they were becoming the norm. Fowler 2-6-2 and 2-6-4 tanks began to arrive, and shortly after that

came the Stanier revolution, with its consequent LNWR blitz. But it did mean variety, as one never quite knew what might appear. Before the war, New Street saw few Pacifics, and indeed they were very rare in later years. In truth, the only really fast trains were those to London.

It was this change-over period that gave me my first LMS footplate ride, on an ex-LNWR 'George the Fifth' class locomotive, but it also cost me a parental fine of a month's pocket money. We had finished school early one day, and I had gone down to New Street to see what was about. I was not really expecting anything too exciting, as in 1937, all the headlines were being made on the Trent Valley line, with the 'Coronation Scot' and streamliners. I was standing on Platform 2, just after lunchtime, when a train came in behind a 'George' class locomotive, but to my lasting shame I can't definitely remember if it was No. 25321 *Lord Loch* or No. 25393 *Loyalty*, but it was almost certainly the latter, and it had express headlamps. This was most unusual, for whilst 'Prince of Wales' class 4-6-0 locomotives were reasonably common, the 4-4-0 locomotives had been ousted, first by Compounds and then almost completely by the new 'Black Five' locomotives. The train was the 2.05 p.m. service to London, stopping at Stechford, Coventry and Rugby before going on to Euston via Northampton. The driver turned out to be an Aston man whom I knew, and who was very much a LNWR stalwart, and after a chat I was offered a ride to Rugby, but not on the main line he said! This was unrefusable and very memorable, but I returned home extremely late. Looking back, apart from the thrill of actually riding on an engine, watching the crew at work en route and the passengers on the stations, the thing I remember most is the speed of the topping up of the tender tank at Coventry. Before we stopped, the fireman was back on the tender to open the tank flap and within seconds, the driver was at the column wheel. Time was of the absolute essence, especially with this old lady and eight bogies. Other footplate trips came eventually, including one on a 'Prince of Wales' Class, No. 25648 *Queen of the Belgians* going north, but the first is always the best.

In the summer, there were frequent Saturday excursions from Birmingham to Blackwell, and it was possible to sit on the embankment and see train after train come pounding up the bank, with various combinations of engines including, of course, the great 0-10-0. Unfortunately, the afternoon sun was invariably tail on to the trains, and photography with an old folding 1A Kodak was hardly worthwhile, something which I now regret. However, it is interesting to note that most of the better pictures taken on the Lickey Incline in the past are on dullish days. Sometimes, we would change trains at King's Norton on the way back, just to have a ride down to New Street via Moseley and Camp Hill, often in a comfortable ex-Midland clerestory coach on a Redditch branch local.

Other trips on Saturdays and summer evenings included runs to Bescot, with its great metal footbridge spanning the bifurcated tracks. This gave excellent views of the shed and the trains moving to and from Wolverhampton, Dudley and Walsall. Saturdays could produce interesting workings, such as an LNWR 'Super D' double-heading a Compound, on diverted trains from the Midland via Wichnor, Lichfield and Walsall. We usually booked a ticket through to Wolverhampton, which allowed us to come back on a fast train via Dudley Port.

New Street was fitted into my adolescent years with greater intensity than Snow Hill, as I spent two years at Birmingham Central Technical College, where the upper floor lecture rooms overlooked the whole complex, with the sound and smell of steam continually floating up towards us. This proximity allowed quick visits during the lunch hour, and allowed one to see just what was working the 6.00 p.m. fast train to Sutton Coldfield. Even in 1938, this was often an LNWR 18in. Watford tank.

Further afield were Lichfield and Rugby, to which visits were kept for holiday times, but they were well worth it. The Birmingham loop was always regarded as a semi-backwater, and we never saw big engines like Pacifics, and the environment did not allow trains to travel fast either. Lichfield Trent Valley, which was reached via Sutton Coldfield or Walsall, provided an excellent day out, as we could log the streamliners rushing through and come home behind either a brand new Stanier 2-6-4 tank via Sutton or a wheezing LNW 'Cauliflower' via Walsall. Rugby, however, was further afield and more expensive, so really warranted a full day's outing. It was here that expresses passed through in procession but some, including blue and silver streamliners, stopped and enabled us to have a good look at these new and fascinating machines. The southern end of the platforms also gave us a view of the shed and, of course, the Great Central's old main line as it crossed the LMS, close to that huge signal gantry. Sometimes, we would go down the road to the quieter LNER island platform station to take a closer look at the 'Director' class 4-4-0 and the new Football Club 4-6-0 locomotives, all of which stopped at Rugby.

Stanier soon brought standardization to the West Midlands main lines, and by 1938, the only pre-grouping express passenger engines which regularly attended New Street were Class 2 4-4-0 locomotives and Compounds on the Midland side, and Bletchley or Stafford 'Prince of Wales' class locomotives on the North-Western, although very occasionally one of Stafford shed's superheated 'Precursor' class, No. 25245 *Antaeus* would put in an appearance. Fortunately, the shed master at Stafford was kindly, and visits there allowed an excellent view of the main line, as well as the facility to be in the centre of a number of the remaining 'George the Fifth' and 'Prince of Wales' class locomotives. The former included

No. 25321 *Lord Loch*, No. 25348 *Coronation*, No. 25393 *Loyalty*, and the latter No. 25648 *Queen of the Belgians*, No. 25674 *Scott*, and Nos. 25725, 25775, 25804 and 25841.

To the north-west of Birmingham was Crewe, very much a holy of holies and only to be visited in parties, unless one was in the know, as was that great doyen of railway photographers, the Manchester-based Will Whitworth. His proud and just boast was that nothing escaped from Crewe Works without it passing the lens of his camera. Will took one of the very few pictures of the new Stanier 2-6-0 which emerged with a Great Western type brass safety valve bonnet, an adornment which was removed extremely quickly once discovered by that great man. The works in those days was a particularly fascinating place to visit, as a whole half century of locomotives could be on view, from the spanking new Pacifics down to Webb 0-6-0 coal engines. There were also a few remaining oddities, like the crane tank in the yard. Sadly, it was also the scene of the holocaust with North Stafford and LNWR engines being scrapped daily. Even more sad was that this was not a period when anyone really considered preservation, and indeed the opposite was the case, with Stanier ordering the destruction of some engines restored and kept at Derby. Crewe made a meagre preservation attempt, in that the authorities hid away the very last superheated 'Precursor', No. 25297 *Sirocco*, and perhaps hoped that something might happen, but it never did. She eventually ended up on the scrap road, marked 'Farewell good and faithful servant'. But that was in the primeval BR times.

Post-war years included a trip on demobilization from Stafford to New Street behind a Class 2P, visits to Dudley Port to see the 'Dudley Dasher', which was a Webb 5ft. 6in. 2-4-2 with its push–pull train, and journeys to see the remaining branches using older motive power. Up until 1948, these older locomotives were still about and at work, for example Midland Class 1F Kirtley outside framed 0-6-0 locomotives working on the Halesowen branch, an open cab MR 0-6-0 tank at Dursley, LNW 2-4-2 and coal tanks at Coalport, and coal tanks and coal engines around Shrewsbury and Minsterley. It was all a mad rush to see them whilst the going was good, with even the petrol rationing authorities agreeing to supply supplementary coupons in order that these relics of the past could be recorded on film. This was something discovered by that doyen Arthur Camwell, and passed on to us with relish, for which we will always be grateful.

Plate 1: Harborne goods yard looking towards Birmingham, showing the coal yard, goods shed, signal box and in the right distance, the then newly-built Chad Valley toy factory.

W. A. Camwell

Plate 2: One of the then new Stanier 2-6-2 tanks, No. 117 leaves Five Ways Station in the summer of 1936, with the 6.43 p.m. Birmingham (New Street) to Redditch local train. The freight train on the upper level is on the goods only line to the Central Goods Station via Granville Street, the original terminus of the Birmingham West Suburban Railway.

P. B. Whitehouse

Plate 3: Waiting on the centre road, with a train for Stafford via Bescot and Wolverhampton, superheated 'Precursor' class 4-4-0, No. 5248 *Amphion* is coaled up, probably at Aston shed, and ready to move into platform No. 1. The picture was taken sometime during 1928/9.

A. W. Flowers

Plate 4: Platform No. 2 at New Street Station, in the summer of 1934, with 18in. goods 0-6-0 locomotives, Nos. 8548 and 8451 in the platform. The latter is heading a Harborne branch local service.

P. B. Whitehouse

Plate 5: Ex-LNWR 'Prince of Wales' class 4-6-0, No. 25725 of Stafford Shed is seen alongside a new LMS 'Black Five', No. 5245, on a summer Saturday in 1938. This was one of the batch of five or so Stafford-based 'Prince of Wales' class locomotives, the remainder being based at Bletchley. The train is the 3.35 p.m. (SO) to Manchester, and is loaded to eight bogies.

P. B. Whitehouse

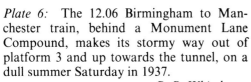

Plate 6: The 12.06 Birmingham to Manchester train, behind a Monument Lane Compound, makes its stormy way out of platform 3 and up towards the tunnel, on a dull summer Saturday in 1937.

P. B. Whitehouse

Plate 7: George Whale's LNWR 'Experiment' class 4-6-0, originally No. 372 *Germanic* of 6/05, is pictured running as LMS No. 5453 *Belgic*. During World War I, the name *Germanic* was considered unpatriotic, and was literally crossed through on the plate, with *Belgic* being stamped over the top. The scene is Handsworth Wood on the LNWR's Soho loop, and the date probably the early 1930s.

P. Gloster collection

Plate 8: Barnt Green Station, in 1936, looking towards Birmingham. On the right is a New Street to Worcester all stations train, headed by an ex-Midland Class 4F 0-6-0 locomotive.

P. B. Whitehouse

Plate 9: Barnt Green Station, in the summer of 1936. These are the platforms for the Redditch branch, the line becoming single once station limits are passed. The train is a mixed freight bound for Washwood Heath sidings via the Camp Hill loop, and is headed by ex-MR Class 3 0-6-0, No. 3520. The platform on the right which contains the station buildings is an island, serving the Worcester and Bristol bound trains on the main line. At this time, express motive power was just changing hands, from 4-4-0 locomotives to the new Stanier 4-6-0 engines.

P. B. Whitehouse

Plate 10 (above): A poor but fascinating picture of an LNWR 'Super D', carrying express headlamps, and double-heading an LMS-built 4-4-0 Compound. It is approaching Bescot Junction on the curve from Walsall, in the spring of 1938. The train has probably come from Derby, and has been diverted via Wichnor Junction, Lichfield and Brownhills. The 0-8-0 will have been needed in view of the climb from Lichfield (City) to Brownhills.

P. B. Whitehouse

Plate 11 (left): A blue and silver 'Princess Coronation' class Pacific, No. 6221 *Queen Elizabeth*, with a northbound express. It is pictured at Rugby in 1938.

P. B. Whitehouse

Plate 12 (right upper): Stafford Shed in the summer of 1939, featuring its twin coaling hoists. The engine is a Crewe-built Bowen-Cooke 4-6-0, No. 25674 *Scott*, one of the shed's two named 'Prince of Wales' class locomotives. The other was No. 25648 *Queen of the Belgians*. On the right is an LMS Class 2P 4-4-0, and the gantry signal is off for a train going out of the bay platform.

P. B. Whitehouse

Plate 13 (right lower): Crewe's 5,000th locomotive was 'George the Fifth' class, LMS No. 25348 *Coronation*, seen underneath the coaling stage at Stafford in 1939. Positioned over the splasher is the unique nameplate with its crown, celebrating the coronation of King George V and below, the acknowledgement that it was indeed the 5,000th locomotive.

P. B. Whitehouse

Plate 14: The 'Royal Scot' on exhibtion at the British Industries Fair at Castle Bromwich, after it had returned from its tour of the USA.

E. Manley, courtesy Warwick County Museum.

Plate 15: A complete LNWR train at Coalport Terminus in 1947, with Webb 5ft. 6in. radial tank, No. 6757 waiting for right away with an afternoon train for Wellington. During that year, three classes of North-Western engine worked the branch, all being Webb types, including 5ft. 6in. 2-4-2 tanks, 0-6-2 coal tanks and a solitary 18in. goods 0-6-0.

P. B. Whitehouse

Plate 16: Webb LNWR coal engine 0-6-0, still without vacuum brakes, on a pick-up freight at Hadley near Wellington, Shropshire in 1947.

P. B. Whitehouse

Chapter Two – NEW STREET STATION

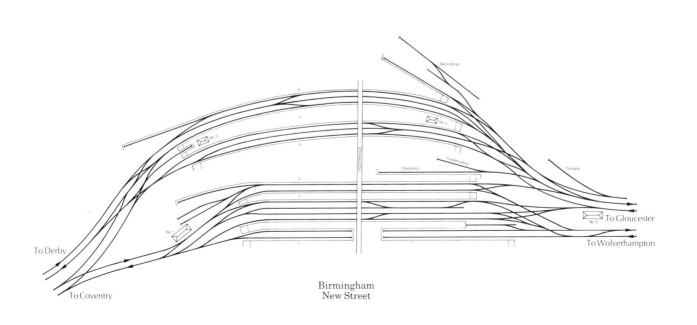

Birmingham
New Street

During the early days of the LMS, the various local services out of the LNWR side of New Street were in the hands of five classes of tank, and one tender engine. These consisted of four Webb engines, including 5ft. 6in. 2-4-2 radial tank, 18in. 0-6-2 'Watfords' and 0-6-2 coal tanks, plus 18in. goods 0-6-0 locomotives, one 'Whale', in the form of the 4-4-2 tanks and, less often, the Bowen-Cooke 4-6-2 tanks. All except the latter were regular performers until the late 1930s, and the earlier Webb classes of 0-6-2 tank were in action as north and south end pilots well into Nationalization.

Plate 17 (below): Pictured just into the Grouping period, a Bowen-Cooke 4-6-2 tank waits in platform 2, with a local train from Coventry. The whole train is still in LNWR colours, with the locomotive, No. 962 of 1912, carrying the full initials on its tank sides. An interesting feature is the loading gauge, overhanging the 'down' main line, adjacent to platform 3. This elliptical roofed bogie stock was to last at least another decade. Other 4-6-2 tanks of this period seen in New Street included Nos. 809, 841, 944, 1797 and 2670.

W. Leslie Good
P. B. Whitehouse Collection

Plate 18 (right upper): In the early days of Grouping, passenger engines were painted red, and carried the LMS Company's crest on their cab sides. This rule was generally applied to main line locomotives for a couple of years or so, and also a few tank engines. Before long, Crewe saw to it that proper LNWR black reappeared, to adorn its own locomotives. One of the rare red tanks was Webb radial, No. 6620, which has just hooked off a local service from Walsall via Aston, and is ready to move off to Monument Lane shed for servicing, in 1926. The first red painted 5ft. 6in. tank to appear at New Street was No. 6707.

P. B. Whitehouse Collection

Plate 19 (right lower): A later photograph than the previous ones, taken well into the 1930s. This Webb 18in. 0-6-2 tank, No. 6923, is probably the north end pilot, carrying shed code No. 3E (Monument Lane). It is still fairly clean, with gold blocked letters and numbers, and would take its turn on passenger duties. In fact, during the late 1930s, one of the these engines regularly worked the fast train of the day to Sutton, Four Oaks and Lichfield, this being the 6.00 p.m. first stop Wylde Green and then all stations service. This provided a real firework display when climbing the 1 in 107 gradient between Erdington and Chester Road stations.

C. F. H. Oldham

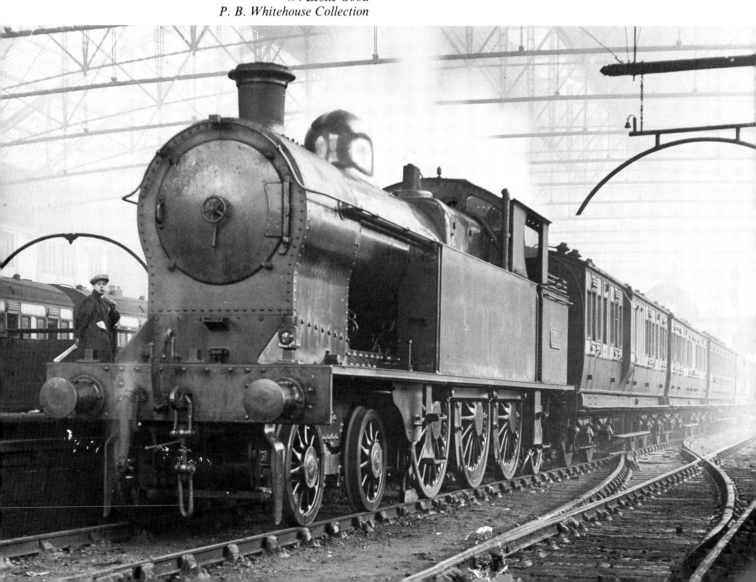

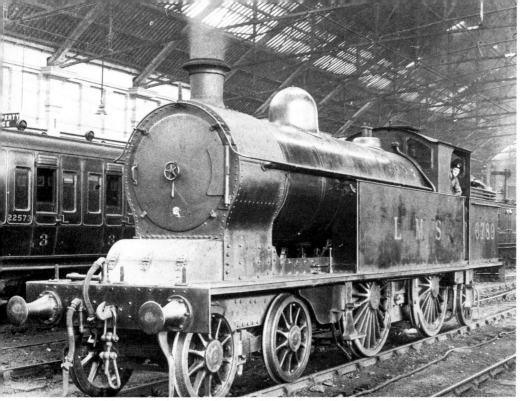

Plate 20: By 1927, most engines and stock were being repainted in the standard LMS colours, with all tank locomotives finished in black. This Whale 4-4-2 'Precursor' class tank appears to have had part of the treatment, as her boiler is still lined out as in LNWR days, whilst her plain black tank and bunker sides wear the new company initials and the number 6789. Shed plate No. 10 indicates that this is an Aston engine, and her main duties included working the Sutton line, as well as Coventry and Leamington local trains.

W. Leslie Good
P. B. Whitehouse Collection

Plate 21: A general view of New Street Station, taken from the south end of platform 2, circa 1928. Alongside the through portion of platform 1 is 'George the Fifth' class 4-4-0, No. 5331 *J. P. Bickersteth*, with a Coventry and Rugby train, the leading vehicle being an LNWR saloon. On the centre road is the south end pilot (this was generally an 0-6-2 coal tank), and behind this, a 4-4-2 'Precursor' class tank stands with empty stock for a Sutton Coldfield and Four Oaks train.

A. W. Flowers

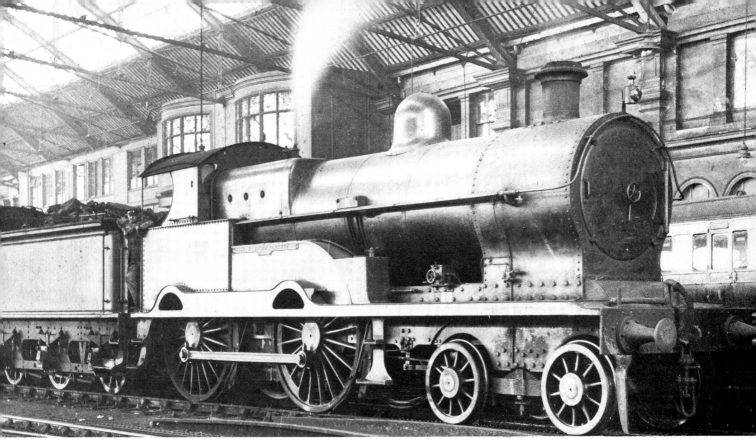

Plate 22: A close up of George the Fifth class 4-4-0, No. 5331 *J. P. Bickersteth*, at New Street Station, Birmingham, in 1930.

A. W. Flowers

Plate 23: The LNWR war memorial 'Claughton' class 4-6-0, No. 5964 *Patriot*, with short wheelbase ex-'R.O.D.' tender and LNER stock, seen standing at the south end of No. 1 main line platform in 1928. It was heading the afternoon train to Harwich via Rugby and Peterborough, this being a regular 'Claughton' duty for some years.

A. W. Flowers

Plate 24: New Street Station, looking south from the end of platform 2 circa 1930, with a Fowler 2-6-2 tank, carrying its original five figure numbering, heading a local train. This evocative shot brings back the atmosphere of the station at the time.

P. B. Whitehouse Collection

Plate 25: New Street Station, showing platform 1 facing platform 2, (old nomenclature) with 'Crab' 2-6-0 on a semi-fast 'up' train, around 1927. On the left are the two No. 1 platform bays, used for Coventry and Walsall local trains.

A. W. Flowers

Plates 26 and 27: Two more pictures of New Street at the end of the period, both showing relics of its past in the form of motive power. The old LNWR station is in the process of being demolished, with the removal of the great overall roof. The central footbridge is still in place and the steelwork for the new canopies has been erected. The south end pilot, as had been the custom for many years, is a Webb 0-6-2 coal tank No. 7759, albeit in its last days. The latter was a Monument Lane engine, and one of two in its class with extended side tanks for use on the Wirral lines. Its headlamps are not class A but are, in fact, a single head and tail lamp. The Midland side was still very much as built and although the old lower quadrant signal arms are gone, the roofless gents toilets have not. The engine, though disfigured by a Stanier chimney, is Class 2P, No. 385, in pure Midland condition.

P. B. Whitehouse and H. C. Casserley

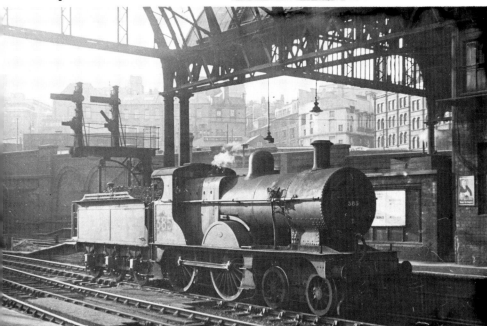

Plate 28 (below): Although five weeks out of period, this photograph, taken on 6th February 1948, shows New Street in its final days of steam, with the old North Western overall roof removed, and new steel canopies fitted over platforms 1 to 3. The train is an 'up' Glasgow to Birmingham service, and 'Royal Scot' class 4-6-0, No. 6158 *The Loyal Regiment*, in new LMS lined out black, is about to depart for Vauxhall carriage sidings and Aston shed.

C. F. H. Oldham

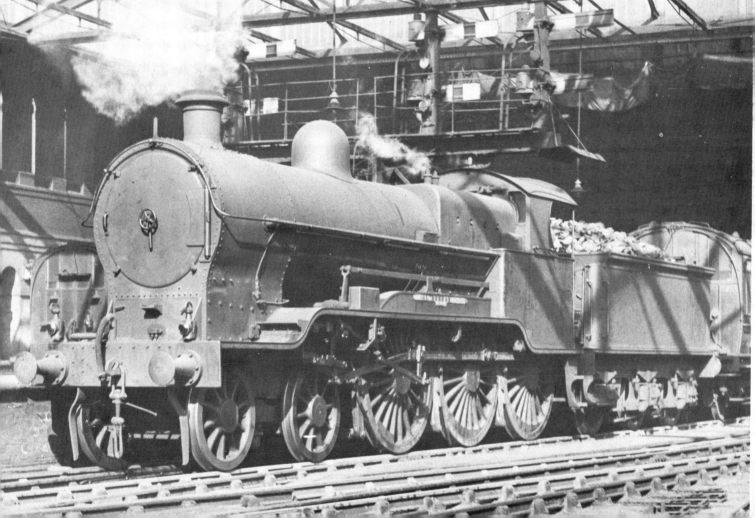

Plate 29 (left upper): An afternoon Liverpool express, waiting in platform 3 at New Street Station, headed by an unnamed, red-painted and re-boilered 'Claughton' class 4-6-0, No. 5962, circa 1928. The sheets under the glass roof are there to catch the debris from the occasional cleaning that takes place. The bracket signal is off for both the main line and the 1 in 77 gradient through the tunnel to Monument Lane; both crew members are looking back waiting for the right away signal.

A. W. Flowers

Plate 30 (left lower): A 'Tishy' 'Prince of Wales' class 4-6-0, No. 5672 *Condor*, with a Manchester via Stoke train in platform 2, pictured in 1928. The engine has been serviced at Aston shed, and will have picked up its train from Vauxhall carriage sidings. Fitted with a Belpaire firebox, and with good thick wheel tyres, the engine is probably not long out of Crewe Works.

A. W. Flowers

Plate 31: A night scene at the north end of platform 3, sometime in 1935. On the left, an unknown 'Prince of Wales' class 4-6-0, still carrying its old LNWR style shed plate No. 10 (Aston), heads a Wolverhampton and Stafford local train. A new and as yet unnamed Stanier 'Jubilee' class 4-6-0, No. 5556, with LMS type shed plate No. 1B (Camden), waits to depart with a London (Euston) to Birmingham and Wolverhampton (High Level) two hour express. The locomotive was later given the name *Nova Scotia*.

F. E. Hemming

Plate 32 (below): A Rugby 4-4-0 Compound, built by the LMS, and photographed at No. 2 platform. This train terminated at Birmingham, and the locomotive is now carrying light engine headlamps, ready to move off for servicing, probably at Monument Lane shed.

N. E. Stead

Plates 33 and 34: Two photographs o ex-LNWR Webb 18in. 0-6-2 tanks, ac ing as north end pilots at New Stre Station, taken some ten years apart. Th first shows No. 6927, waiting at th advance starting signal, with parcel van in 1937. On the right of the picture i the signal controlling the exit from th LNW lines to the Midland ones, and th bracket giving access to platforms No 4 and 5. The second shows a grimy N 6900, on the same duty in 1947. Th class did not become extinct for anothe six years.

P. B. Whitehous

Plate 35 (below): Ex-Midland 2-4-0, No. 129, acting as south end pilot in 1925. Still resplendent in Midland red, this Kirtley (re-built by Johnson) engine of 1874 was one of the class of twenty engines with smaller 6ft. 3in. driving wheels. The train is standing in platform 4 at around 11.20 in the morning, and is probably collecting milk empties for return to the Tamworth area. The station advertisements include Foster Clarks Cream Custard, Swan Pens and Dri-Ped. The poster boards are still headed Midland, L&NWR and GWR.

A. W. Flowers

The 'new' or Midland side of New Street was the last to retain its overall roof, before demolition and rebuilding took place. The two stations were separated by a roadway known as Queen's Drive, and joined together for passenger ex-change by a footbridge, which was not only covered but also contained two small shops. This was always the quieter side of New Street because trains were less frequent and the engines smaller and less interesting, in that they were not named, for example.

Plate 36: A veteran locomotive, this being old Midland railway No. 1–A Kirtley double-framed 2-4-0, of 1866, in the role of west end pilot at New Street in 1928. The engine is pictured in the early LMS red livery, with the crest on the cabside but with a standard Midland cast-iron number plate on the smokebox door, and large numerals on the tender. The shed plate No. 3 indicates Saltley, but the engine was actually sub-shedded at Bournville. This locomotive was often used on the Birmingham West Suburban line local trains, running via Five Ways, Church Road and Somerset Road for Bournville and King's Norton. It was withdrawn in 1930, and restored to its former Midland state as No. 156A for preservation purposes, but was subsequently broken up during the Stanier holocaust.

A. W. Flowers

Plate 37: During the period, after the disgrace of the 0-6-4 tanks and before Stanier 2-6-2 tanks were in plentiful supply, a number of smaller ex-London Tilbury & Southend 4-4-2 tanks were moved to the Birmingham area. They were redundant due to their replacement by Stanier 2-6-4 tanks, and were mainly used on the Redditch services. One of these locomotives, No. 2105, is seen at New Street Station.

P. B. Whitehouse Collection

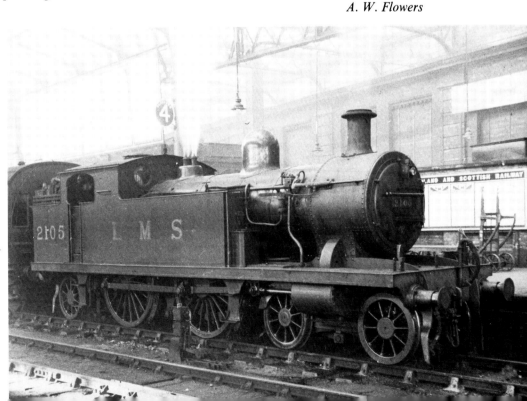

Plate 38: A Gloucester shedded, Midland-built Compound, No. 1025 backs on to a York to Bristol express train, headed by a Stanier 'Black Five', at the west end of No. 6 platform on 7th February 1945, both engines painted in wartime unlined black. Note the war-damaged glassless roof, and the parcel bays to the right of the picture.

C. F. H. Oldham

Chapter Three – GRAND JUNCTION AND SOUTH STAFFS

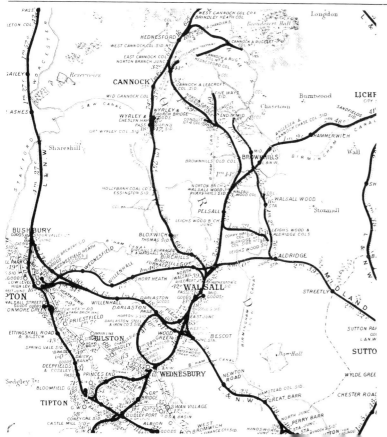

Plate 39 (right below): The track layout, south of New Street Tunnel, looking towards Proof House Junction. The old Curzon Street terminus of the London & Birmingham Railway can be seen on the left of the picture. At the time, when nationalization was imminent, not only the original building but also the train shed were still standing, with the whole scene, including signals, reflecting London & North Western style and practices.

J. C. Flemons

Plate 40 (right lower): With LMS upper quadrant signals in view this photograph, taken from the balcony of Proof House Junction signal box, clearly shows the approaches to Birmingham from the south. On the extreme left are the tracks into Curzon Street Yard. Climbing up and over the complex layout is the Grand Junction line to Wolverhampton or Walsall both via Bescot, and branching off at Aston, the Sutton Coldfield and Lichfield line. Right centre in the LNWR main line to Coventry and beyond, whilst on the right are the old Midland tracks from Derby or, via the Lifford loop, from King's Norton and the south-west.

J. C. Flemons

Plate 41: Webb 18in. goods engine No. 8482 sits outside Aston shed, some time in 1934. At the time, the Stanier engines were only just beginning to appear, and the class was still in service on local trains, particularly those to Walsall and, prior to November of that year, over the Harborne branch.

W. Leslie Goo[...]

Plate 42 (below): Aston shed in 193[...] with the then new Stanier 2-6-4 tank No. 2611 outside. In the background [...] 'Jinty' 0-6-0 tank, No. 7366 and a[n] unknown ex-LNWR 0-6-2 coal tank.

P. B. Whitehous[...]

Plate 43: A classic example of LNWR standardization, left in situ by the LMS is the building on the 'up' platform a[t] Four Oaks Station, on the Sutton Coldfield to Lichfield City line. With only minor modifications, it exists to this day though BR has replaced a somewha[t] similar building on the 'down' platform with a glass bus shelter.

E. S. Russel[l]

Plate 44: Penns for Walmley Station, on the one-time Midland branch, with Fowler 2-6-4T, No 2337 arriving with the 5.35 p.m. train from Birmingham to Walsall, via Sutton Park.

E. S. Russell

Plate 45: Streetly Station, located on the ex-Midland Railway branch from Castle Bromwich to Walsall and Wolverhampton. Class 4F, No. 4069 is seen waiting with a Sunday ballast train.

E. S. Russell

Plate 46 (below): Stanier 2-6-4 tank, No. 2482 heads the 1.45 p.m. (SO) Walsall to Birmingham train, pictured at Sutton Park. An ex-LNWR twelve wheeled dining saloon, relegated to departmental use, is just visible to the left of the signal box.

E. S. Russell

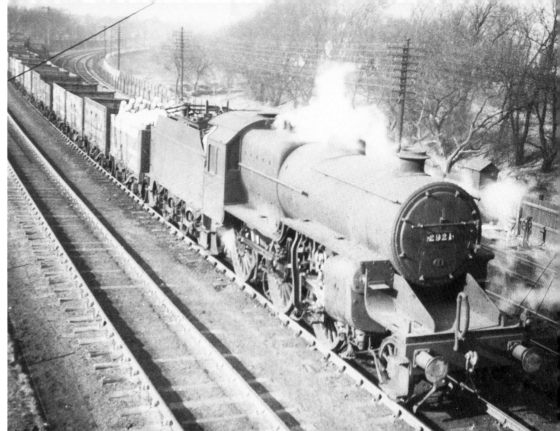

Plate 50: A Fowler 2-6-0 'Crab', No. 2921, approaches Bescot Junction, with a long freight train from the Dudley line, one afternoon in the spring of 1938.

P. B. Whitehouse

Plate 51: Bescot Junction, looking towards Birmingham, photographed in 1938. The train , behind 2-6-4 tank, No. 2487, is bound for Walsall, and the locomotive shed is to the right of the picture.

P. B. Whitehouse

Plate 52: Bescot shed dump, on 7th April 1928, with two ex-LNWR freight engines still carrying their old numbers and livery. The 0-8-0 tender engine is No. 1606 and the tank is an 0-8-2, No. 1414, which was an unusual visitor to the Birmingham area. In the distance is the locomotive shed, still with its north light roof, and a row of Webb engines awaiting repair. Bescot was capable of undertaking a greater volume of repairs than other ex-LNW sheds in the district, possessing a wheel, axle, and crank pin turning lathe, as well as the necessary machine tools to deal with axleboxes and the usual wheel drop.

C. J. Nevitt

Plate 53: Bescot shed in 1947, which was the final home of the LNWR 'Super D' class 0-8-0 locomotives which by that date were carrying Stanier chimneys. The last serving engines were withdrawn from here in 1964.

P. B. Whitehouse

Plate 54: Walsall shed 3C (Ryecroft), pictured in the 1930s. The LNWR 5ft. 6in. radial tank, No. 6685, although carrying the later cast-iron shed code plate, is still painted in early LMS livery, with the crest on the bunker side. This auto-fitted engine worked the Wolverhampton to Bescot, Walsall to Dudley, and the Dudley to Dudley Port services, and after a long life was still in service at Walsall in 1945. *W. Leslie Good*

Plate 55 (below): Ex-Midland Railway 2-4-0, pictured as LMS No. 20008, (Previously No. 8) standing outside Walsall (Ryecroft) shed, on 3rd October 1937. The old Midland shed at Pleck East Junction had closed in 1925, with the MR line from Wolverhampton to Walsall being transferred to Western Division supervision in 1927.

P. M. Alexander

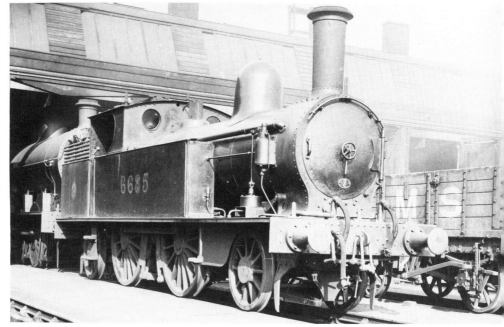

Plate 56 (right upper): Ex-LNWR Webb 2-4-2 tank, No. 6757 waits at Walsall, with a train for Dudley via Great Bridge and Dudley Port (Low Level).

E. S. Russell

Plate 57 (right lower): Caught by the camera, at Great Bridge Station, ex-LNWR Webb 2-4-2 tank No. 6757 waits with a Walsall to Dudley train. The notice on top of the old LNWR goods shed reads London Midland and Scottish Railway Goods Department. Passenger traffic was not heavy, and a Walsall bound customer is sleeping away the time, on the slatted wooden platform seat, while he waits for his train.

E. S. Russell

Chapter Four – HARBORNE

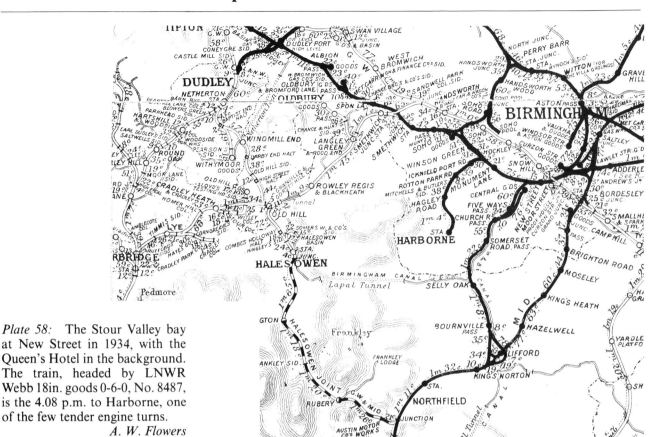

Plate 58: The Stour Valley bay at New Street in 1934, with the Queen's Hotel in the background. The train, headed by LNWR Webb 18in. goods 0-6-0, No. 8487, is the 4.08 p.m. to Harborne, one of the few tender engine turns.

A. W. Flowers

Plate 59: Although Monument Lane Shed was geographically nearest to the branch, Harborne trains tended to be worked by Aston and Walsall engines. LNWR tanks 4-4-2, No. 6883 and 0-6-2, No. 6782 sit behind the shed, during May 1937. It is likely that the 4-4-2 tank has come up from Rugby or Coventry, as during the last years of their existence, few were shedded in the Birmingham area.

G. S. Lloyd

Plates 60, 61, 62, 63, & 64: A selection of views of Rotton Park Road Station, taken during the last week of passenger operation in November 1934. This was the only passing place on the line, and the intermediate block post between Harborne Junction and Harborne. The staffs in the single line apparatus are marked Harborne Junction and Rotton Park Road. The locomotive in both photographs is ex-LNWR 0-6-2 radial tank, No. 6924 running chimney first to Harborne, not being turned for the Birmingham bound journey.

W. A. Camwell

Plate 65 (right): Another view of Rotton Park Road Station in the early 1930s, showing the approach footbridge and the starter, in the off position, for a Harborne bound train. The catch point for the sand drag, which is clearly shown in the close up photograph of the platform, is to protect the section to Harborne Junction, as the descending gradient from Hagley Road was 1 in 66.

P. B. Whitehouse Collection

Plate 66: Hagley Road Station, on 24th November 1934, the last day of passenger working. The locomotive, No. 7742 is an ex-LNWR 0-6-2 coal tank, one of the regular branch engines, shown with the 1.50 p.m. train from Harborne. This engine worked the last passenger train, this being the 11.15 p.m. (SO) from New Street.

W. A. Camwell

Plates 67 & 68 (right upper): LNWR engines worked most of the Harborne freight services, until their departure from Monument Lane for the scrap-yard. Both these pictures of 0-6-2 tank, No. 6927, were taken from the Woodbourne Road bridge, showing the outward and return trips.

P. B. Whitehouse

Plate 69: An empty evening freight train from Harborne climbs the 1 in 66 gradient towards Woodbourne Road, behind Webb 18in. goods 0-6-0, No. 28616, in July 1949.

T. J. Edgington

Plate 70: Harborne Station on 24th November 1934, this being the last day of passenger working. Only one of the two signals (starter and home) can be seen, along with the footbridge which was used as a pedestrian right of way.

W. A. Camwell

Plate 71: Another last day photograph, showing a very dirty 18in. goods 0-6-0 on the turntable. This worked one of the few trains running through New Street, this being the 2.59 p.m. to Walsall.

W. A. Camwell

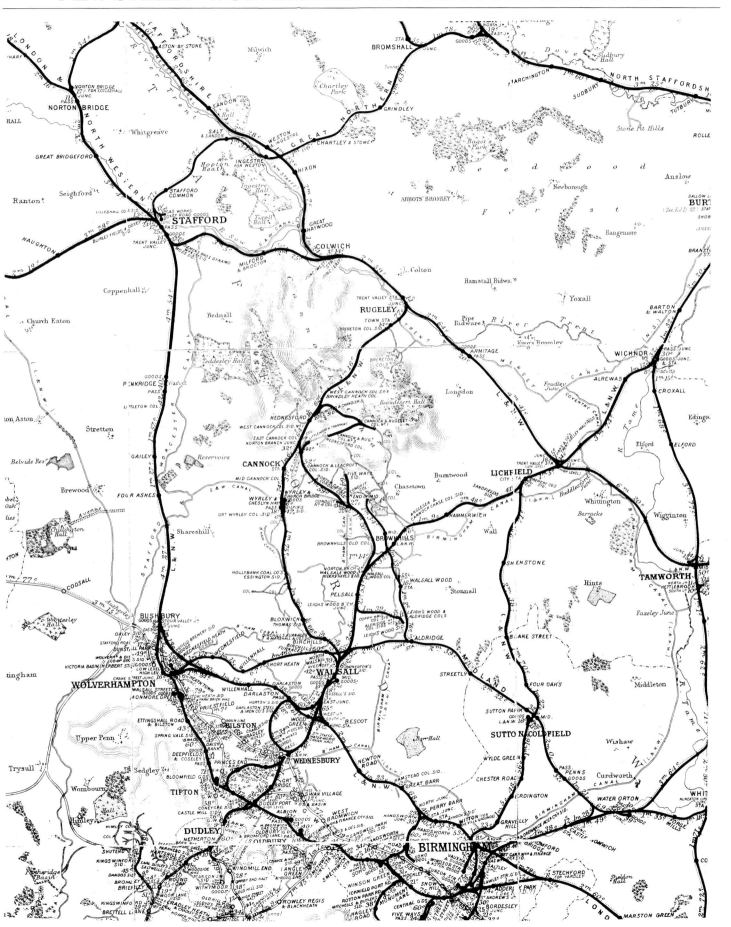

Plate 72 (left): Dudley Port Station in 1947, with the Dudley push-pull train waiting behind LNWR Webb 2-4-2 tank, No. 6712. Dudley Port was a mandatory stop for all expresses both 'up' and 'down', until the coming of electrification and closure of the Dudley branch. During long waits, the whole train was often used to shunt the red Palethorpes 'sausage' vans, in the lower South Staffs yard.

P. B. Whitehouse

Plate 73 (right): LNWR Webb 18in. 0-6-2 tank No. 6900 at Dudley Port late in 1947, working as the Tipton shunter,. This was her last duty before withdrawal from Monument Lane Shed.

P. B. Whitehouse

Plate 74: An unnamed 'Patriot' class 4-6-0, waiting for an 'up' express train, on the centre tracks of Wolverhampton (High Level) Station. The engine is No. 5526 which was, in 1936, a regular performer on the London trains.

P. B. Whitehouse

Plate 75: Ex-LNWR Class G2 0-8-0, shunting at Wolverhampton (High Level) Station in 1936. Note the driver, high up on the step on the side of the footplate, probably frozen on one side and roasted on the other.

P. B. Whitehouse

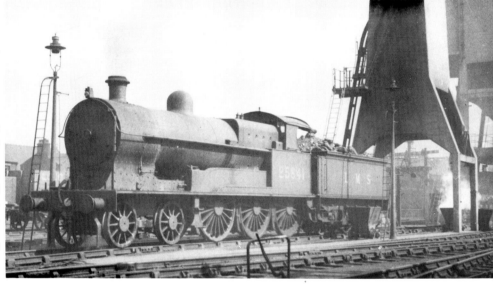

Plates 76, 77 & 78: Stafford Shed was home to LNWR 4-6-0 locomotives during their last decade. They worked a variety of local trains on the main line, and one or two expresses to and from Birmingham, including the 9.45 a.m. New Street to Stafford and Stoke service. Locomotives on shed during this summer day in 1939 included 'George the Fifth' class 4-4-0 locomotives No. 25321 *Lord Loch*, No. 25348 *Coronation*, No. 25393 *Loyalty*, 'Prince of Wales' class 4-6-0 locomotives No. 25648 *Queen of the Belgians*, Nos. 25725 and 25841, and 'Super D' 0-8-0, No. 8918, still with her LNWR chimney.

P. B. Whitehouse

Plate 79: Stanier 'Jubilee' class 4-6-0, No. 5669 *Fisher*, outside the original LNWR shed at Stafford, in 1939.

P. B. Whitehouse

Plate 80: Stafford Station, looking from the locomotive shed yard, during the summer of 1939. The train is the 5.50 p.m. semi-fast to Stoke, stopping at Stoke only, and the engine is one of the few remaining ex-LNWR 'George the Fifth' class 4-4-0 locomotives, No. 25393 *Loyalty*, still with gold shaded numerals and soon for withdrawal. It had taken over from 'Prince of Wales' class 4-6-0, No. 25775, which worked the 4.35 p.m. service from Birmingham.

P. B. Whitehouse

Plate 81 (below): Stafford Station, in August 1939. 'Royal Scot' class, No. 6159 *The Royal Air Force* trails a new Stanier high-capacity tender and waits to back down on to a Rugby to Liverpool train with an extra coach. Locomotives have been changed here, with Beardmore 'Prince of Wales' class, No. 25752 having left the train. On the right is an unknown Fowler class 4F 0-6-0, and 'George the Fifth' class 4-4-0, No. 25348 *Coronation*.

P. B. Whitehouse

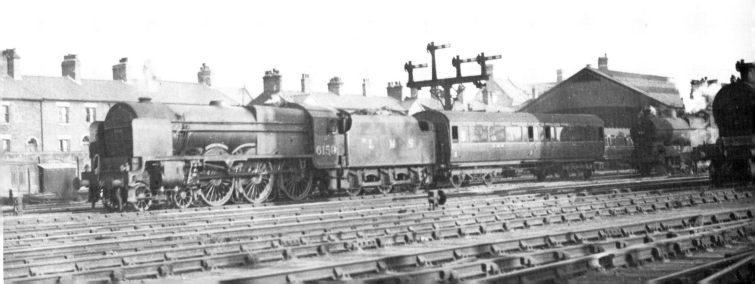

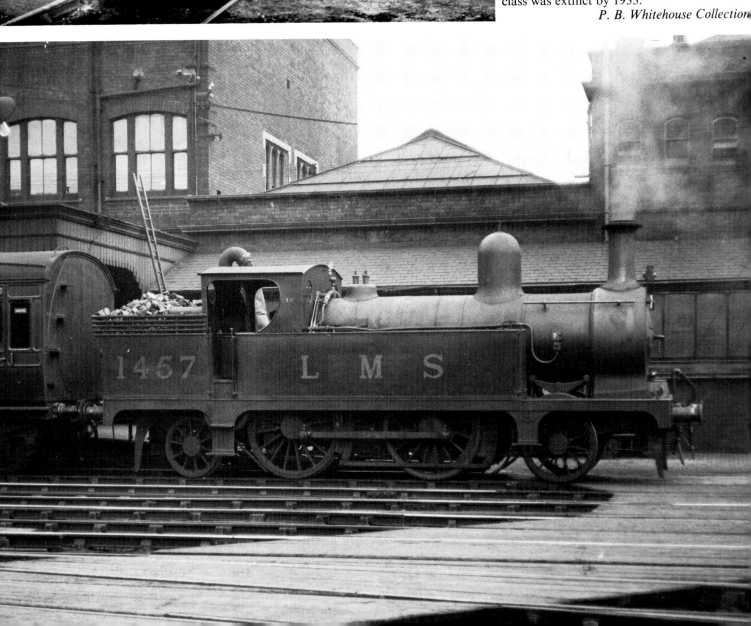

Plate 82: Stanier 'Black Five', No. 5338 takes a fast freight train through Stafford, in August 1939.

P. B. Whitehouse

Plates 83, 84, & 85: Three North Stafford engines, seen working around 1930. Seen at the Stafford end of Stoke Station, the 2-4-2 tank, No. 1457 was one of a class of eight originally built as 2-4-0 tanks between 1878 and 1882, but later rebuilt by Longbottom. Six entered LMS service, but all were gone by 1934. The 0-6-2 tank, No. 2270 is seen sitting on Crewe South Shed, this being one of the four engines actually built in LMS days, in 1923. The 4-4-0, which was renumbered in the 5410-14 series in 1928 to make way for the new LMS Midland type Class 2Ps, dates from 1910-12, and is pictured standing at Crewe North Shed. Sadly, the last figure of the cabside number is not decipherable and the class was extinct by 1933.

P. B. Whitehouse Collection

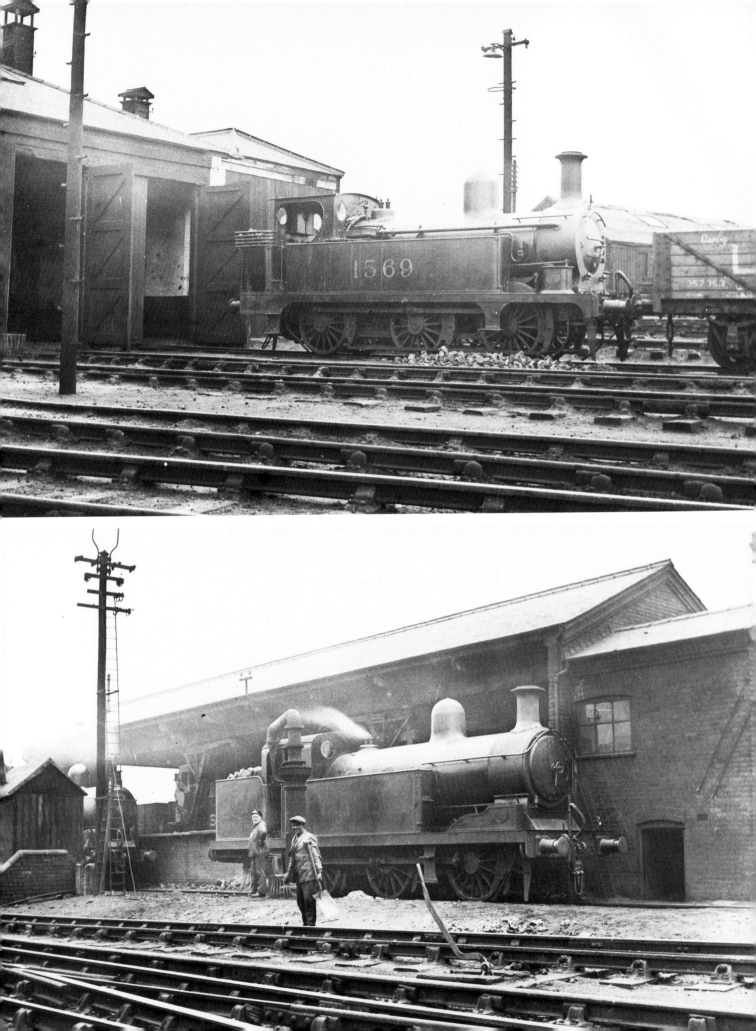

Plate 86 (left upper): Stoke Shed in 1931, with North Stafford 0-6-0 tank, No. 1569, one of a class designed by Longbottom, and built between 1882 and 1899. The last of the class was withdrawn in 1937.

J. A. G. H. Coltas

Plate 87 (left lower): Stoke Shed on the same day, showing Adams 0-6-2 tank, No. 2249 alongside the coaling stage.

J. A. G. H. Coltas

Plate 88 (above): A line up of ex-North Stafford tank engines outside Stoke shed in 1932. The leading engine is No. 2253. Several of this class were purchased for colliery use, and one is now preserved.

J. A. G. H. Coltas

Plate 89 (below): An unusual part of the LMS scene was the narrow gauge railway. A 2ft. 6in. ex-Leek & Manifold Valley Light Railway train stands at Waterhouses narrow/standard gauge exchange station, behind 2-6-4 tank, No. 2 *J. B. Earle*, on 29th April 1933. The last standard gauge passenger train ran on 28th September 1935, while the L&MVR closed on 12th March 1934.

H. C. Casserley

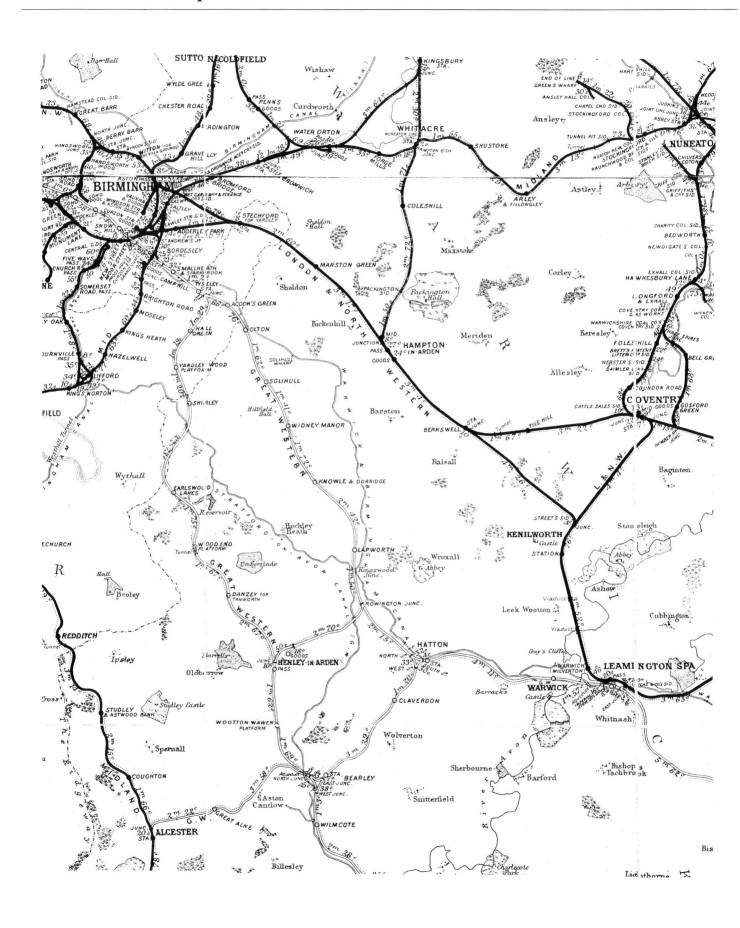

Plate 90: Hampton in Arden Station, looking towards Birmingham, on the New Street to Coventry main line, pictured in 1935. This superseded the old Hampton Station, located to the north of the cutting, which was once a four platformed affair with a junction to Whitacre, on the Midland's line from Derby.

P. Hopkins

Plate 91: A 'down' Birmingham express train, headed by LMS-built Compound 4-4-0, No. 1111, photographed near Hampton in Arden circa 1929, when these engines were the mainstay of the two hour trains.

W. Leslie Good

Plate 92: Still carrying the old 'Claughton' class number 5902, and name *Sir Frank Ree*, one of the first 'Patriot' class locomotives, supposedly rebuilt from an original Claughton heads a two hour express near Hampton in Arden. The train is a motley collection of wooden stock, headed by an ex-LNWR six wheel bogie diner. The date is probably 1930, when the engine was new. This was one of the few locomotives which actually used some 'Claughton' parts, for example the driving wheels with the large bosses.

W. Leslie Good

Plate 93: Berkswell Station, looking towards Birmingham, as seen in 1934. This was the junction for Kenilworth, Warwick (Milverton) and Leamington (Avenue).

P. Hopkins

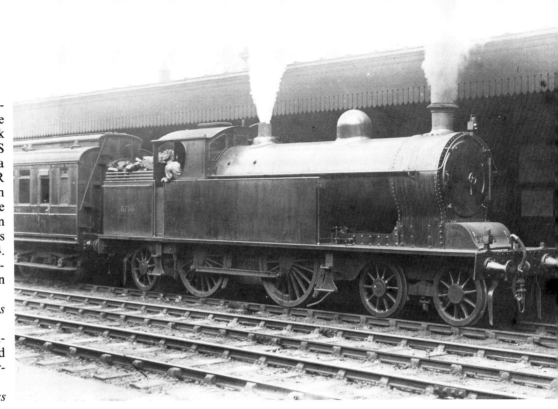

Plate 94: Coventry Station, photographed around 1927. The one-time LNWR 'Precursor' class 4-4-2 tank shows no sign of her new LMS ownership, only indications of a hurried renumbering. The LNWR cast plate has been removed from the bunker, and careful study of the photograph shows faint markings on the paint where it was attached. In its place are the stencilled figures 6794. The coach is an ex-Midland clerestory corridor type which makes an interesting combination.

A. W. Flowers

Plate 95: Two LMS-built Compound locomotives, Nos. 1130 and 1129, heading an 'up' semi-fast service at Coventry in 1927.

A. W. Flowers

Coventry–Nuneaton

Plate 96 (left upper): LNWR 'Experiment' class 4-6-0, No. 5554 *Prospero* is shown here entering Coventry Station, with a 'down' freight, sometime in 1928. The engine, one of George Whale's two cylinder simples, was rebuilt as a four cylinder simple in 1915. This rebuilding did not prove to be successful, and no further members of the class were converted. Dendy Marshall valve gear later replaced the original Joy gear. The whole class, comprising 105 engines, was withdrawn between 1925 and 1935.

A. W. Flowers

Plate 97 (left lower): A 'down' Euston to Birmingham two hour express train enters Coventry Station, circa 1927 headed by LMS-built 4-4-0 Compound, No. 1165. It is a dining car train, the third vehicle being an ex-LNWR restaurant car. To the right of the signal box is the Kenilworth, Warwick and Leamington branch. The engine was virtually new at the time, having been built in September 1925.

A. W. Flowers

Plate 98 (above): A Nuneaton to Coventry and Leamington train, leaving Foleshill during 1937 behind Stanier 2-6-2 tank, No. 109. *A. W. Flowers*

Plate 99 (below): Stanier 2-6-2 tank, No. 143 heads a Nuneaton to Coventry train, seen at Hawkesbury Lane Station, close to nationalization. This line is still open for freight and occasionally for passenger trains, if the main line from Coventry to Birmingham is closed. *E. S. Russell*

Coventry–Leamington

Plate 100: An ex-LNWR 18in. goods 0-6-0 engine, and a Midland Class 4F 0-6-0 locomotive, run light engine double-headed through Kenilworth Station, during 1937. Note the LNWR signal box, perched high to enable signal men to have a clear view over the footbridge.

Roger Carpenter Collection

Plate 101: Pictured with a double-ended push-pull train is ex-LNWR Webb 5ft. 6in. 2-4-2 tank, No. 6653, seen at Kenilworth in 1938. Note the plush interior of the first class compartments.

J. A. G. H. Coltas

Plate 102: One of the last superheated LNWR 'Precursor' class 4-4-0 locomotives No. 25319 *Bucephalus*, seen with a Leamington to Coventry stopping train at Kenilworth Station, in 1938. Note that, although the driver is at his controls, on the left-hand side of the footplate, it is the fireman who is bending out, looking for the guard's 'right away' flag. In spite of its age, No. 25319 was still a regular engine on the afternoon Birmingham to Harwich service, running via Rugby and Peterborough.

J. A. G. H. Coltas

Plate 103: Pictured while carrying express headlamps, ex-LNWR superheated 'Precursor' class 4-4-0, No. 25300 *Hydra* from Rugby Shed waits at Kenilworth Junction, to take the single line to Coventry, sometime in the summer of 1934. To the left is the cut-off line to Birmingham, via Berkswell. The Coventry branch was originally a London & Birmingham protégé, built to keep the GWR out of Coventry, a scheme mooted by the 1844 Oxford & Rugby broad gauge line, which was a GWR subsidiary company. It was planned to bridge the gap between the GWR and L & B main lines from Oxford through Banbury and Southam, with possible extensions to Manchester. This was one of the failures to break the LNWR monopoly at Coventry. Although nothing came of the railway, the GWR obviously had hopes, as they built a hotel in Coventry in anticipation.

Arnold Stringer, M. Musson Collection

Plates 104 & 105: Two ex-LNWR engines, near Warwick (Milverton) in 1932. One is the push-pull service from Coventry, with a Webb 2-4-2 radial tank providing the power, and the other is a local service from Birmingham via Berkswell and Kenilworth, headed by Whale 4-4-2 tank, No. 6824. This was one of the last of her class, but with seven more years of life to go.

Roger Carpenter Collection

Plate 106 (above): One of the ubiquitous ex-LNWR 'Super D' 0-8-0 locomotives, No. 8910, now with a Stanier chimney, seen near Warwick (Milverton) in 1947.

Roger Carpenter Collection

Plate 107: Ex-LNWR Webb 18in goods 0-6-0 locomotive No. 8556, pictured with a mineral train at Warwick (Milverton) Station, in 1937. Note the wheelbarrow, full of coal, for the waiting-room and station staff fireplaces.

J. A. G. H. Coltas

Plate 108: In the 1930s, the Fowler 2-6-2 tanks replaced a number of the ex-LNWR Whale 4-4-2 tanks in the Birmingham division. Heading a local passenger train to Coventry is Fowler 2-6-2 tank No. 3, of the earlier 155xx series. It is crossing over the viaduct at Princes Drive, Leamington, in November 1938.

J. A. G. H. Coltas

Plate 109: A non auto-fitted LNWR Webb 5ft. 6in. 2-4-2 radial tank, allocated to No. 2D shed (Nuneaton) at Leamington (LMS) Station in 1947. The engine is two branch lines away from home, and will have arrived at Leamington via Foleshill, Coventry, Kenilworth and Warwick.

N. J. Allcock

Plate 110: Leamington (LMS) Station, in the summer of 1947, with a very dirty ex-LNWR Webb 5ft. 6in. 2-4-2 tank, No. 6683 on a push-pull train for Daventry and Weedon, both on the Euston main line.

P. B. Whitehouse

Plate 111: A stranger at Leamington (LMS) Station, in 1947. Stafford-based 'Prince of Wales' class, No. 25648 *Queen of the Belgians*, is seen running light engine to Milverton Shed in order to turn. She would then go back with the 5.53 p.m. service to Coventry, then travelling non-stop to Birmingham (New Street).

Roger Carpenter Collection

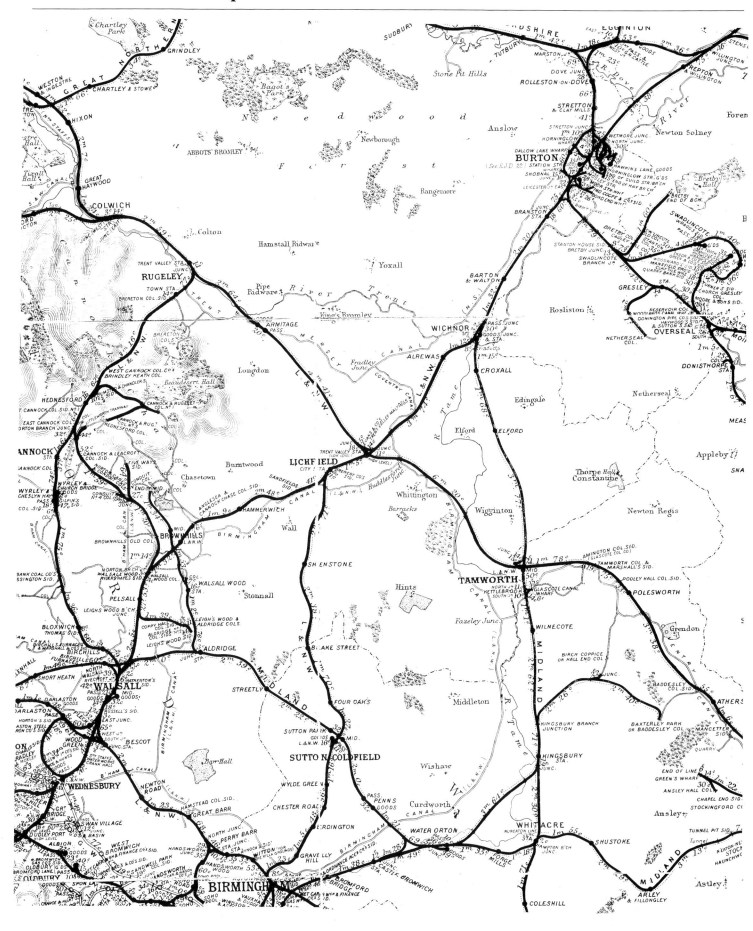

Plate 112: The Birmingham to Derby main line, as seen from the bridge over Landor Street, looking towards Landor Street Junction signal box and Saltley. On the left is Lawley Street goods yard and in front of this are the remains of the connecting viaduct which was opened in 1851 and brought the Midland Railway into Curzon Street. In the centre is Saltley Gas Works and loco shed, and behind the signal box is the Camp Hill line to St. Andrews Junction.

P. B. Whitehouse

Plate 113 (left): The main line from Derby, passing under the old LNWR tracks from London, with the remains of the old connecting viaduct on the right.

J. C. Flemmons
P. B. Whitehouse Collection

Plate 114: Saltley Shed in 1931, with Midland Class 3 4-4-0, No. 711 taking water alongside the old coaling stage. Although painted black, the engine still carries its old safety-valves and bogie brakes. After the tank has been filled, the engine will move forward to be coaled by means of the small tubs, which were all loaded by hand.

W. Leslie Good
P. B. Whitehouse Collection

Plate 115 (left upper): Washwood Heath sidings, on the Midland line out of Birmingham, pictured in the early 1930s. In the background are various MR 0-6-0 locomotives, and the only real sign of Grouping is an LMS 2-6-0 + 0-6-2 'Garratt'.
W. Leslie Good
P. B. Whitehouse Collection

Plate 116 (left lower): A local train, leaving Whitacre Junction just after Grouping. The engine is an MR Kirtley outside-framed 2-4-0, No. 19, from No. 3 shed (Saltley). The single line in the background is the branch to Hampton in Arden, on the old London and Birmingham main line, closed to passengers in 1917, and worked as two sidings from 1930.
W. Leslie Good
P. B. Whitehouse Collection

Plate 117 (right): The Whitacre to Hampton branch, as seen from the Birmingham to Coventry Road photographed around 1940.
P. Hopkins

Plate 118 (below): Wilnecote Station, on the MR Derby to Birmingham line. The engine is Class 5XP 4-6-0, No. 5696 *Arethusa*, on the 1.05 p.m. Newcastle to Bristol express train, pictured passing under the A5 road.
E. S. Russell

Plate 119: Burton-on-Trent Shed in 1925, displaying ex-Midland engines that include Class 4F 0-6-0, No. 4125, a saturated Class 2P, possibly No. 368 and a Class 3F 0-6-0, No. 3205.

A. W. Flowers

Plate 120: Kirtley double-framed 2-4-0, No. 2, inside Burton-on-Trent Shed in 1926.

H. C. Casserley

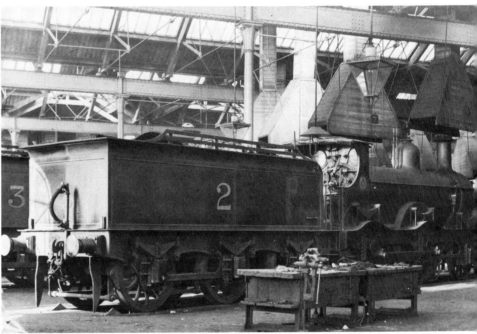

Plate 121: The locomotive portrayed is not LMS, but it was constantly seen at Burton-on-Trent during this period. It is Bass Brewery locomotive No. 11, an 0-4-0 saddle tank by Neilson Reid & Co., in pristine condition.

P. B. Whitehouse

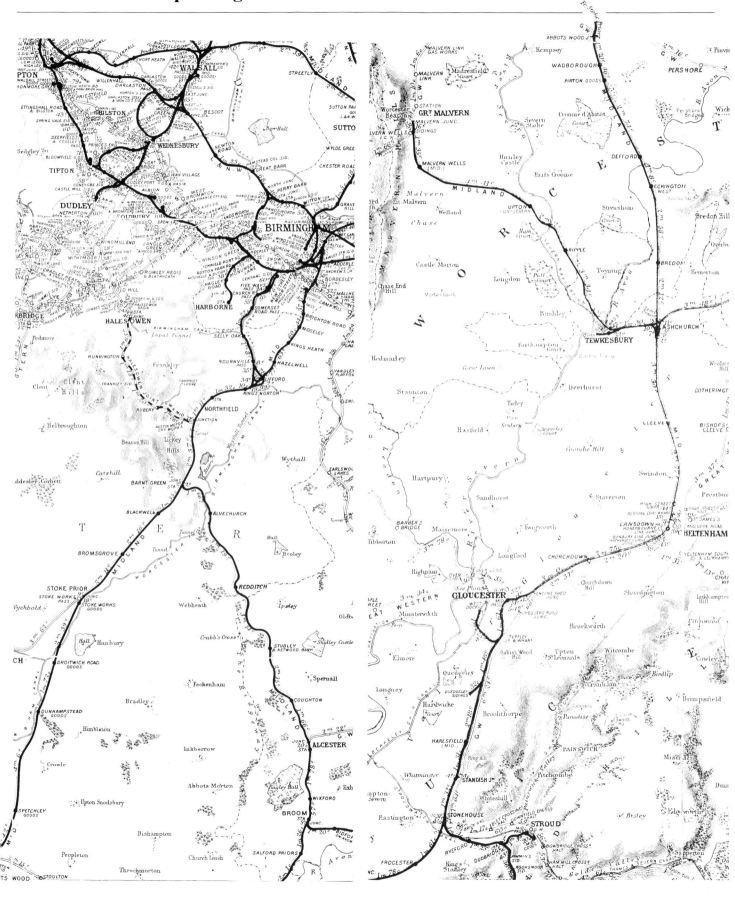

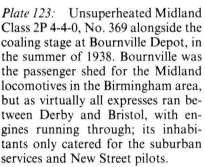

Plate 122: Ex-Midland Railway Class 1F 0-6-0 tank, No. 1700 is seen shunting on the freight only line to Central goods yard. Taken from the footbridge at Five Ways Station, in the summer of 1936.

P. B. Whitehouse

Plate 125 (right upper): Bournville was also home for the Deeley 0-6-4 tanks, colloquially known as 'flat irons' or 'hole in the wall' tanks. These clockwork-looking machines worked the Birmingham Ashchurch trains via Barnt Green, Redditch and Evesham and had a propensity to roll and jump track, being withdrawn as soon as the Stainer 2-6-2 tanks were available. Standing in a line of dead engines is No. 2033, awaiting the end of a short life, after a rebuild with Belpaire firebox and superheater. The photograph was taken around 1936.

W. Leslie Good
P. B. Whitehouse Collection

Plate 123: Unsuperheated Midland Class 2P 4-4-0, No. 369 alongside the coaling stage at Bournville Depot, in the summer of 1938. Bournville was the passenger shed for the Midland locomotives in the Birmingham area, but as virtually all expresses ran between Derby and Bristol, with engines running through; its inhabitants only catered for the suburban services and New Street pilots.

P. B. Whitehouse

Plate 124: One of the double-framed MR Kirtley 2-4-0s, No. 20002, outside Bournville Shed in 1935. This engine was, at the time, one of the regular south end pilots on the Midland side of New Street.

H. C. Casserley

Plate 126 (right lower): In immaculate condition, MR 0-6-4 tank, No. 2025 waits at King's Norton Station, with a Redditch to Birmingham train around 1929. Clerestory stock was still in use on the branch until the late 1930s.

W. Leslie Good
P. B. Whitehouse Collection

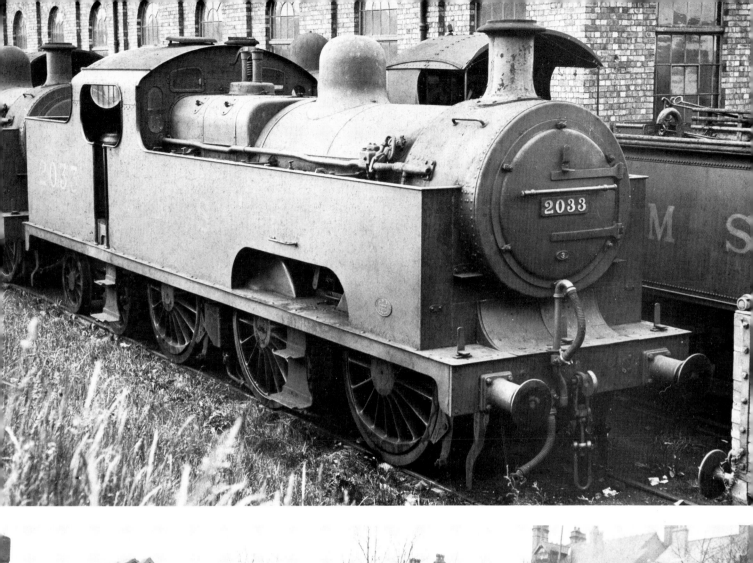

Plate 129 (above): A Johnson 0-4-4 tank, No. 1387 takes a 'down' local train of close coupled ex-Midland stock, between Northfield and Halesowen Junction, during the mid-1920s. Note the LMS crest on the bunker side, and the neatly stacked coal round the rails.
W. Leslie Good
P. B. Whitehouse Collection

Plate 130 (below): One of the Midland's Kirtley 800 class of 6ft. 8½in. double-framed 2-4-0 locomotives of 1870/74, now numbered 60, passes Halesowen Junction after the widening of 1929 had been completed. The train is a 'down' local, and the photograph was taken from the World War I platform built for the Austin Works.
W. Leslie Good
P. B. Whitehouse Collection

Plate 127 (left upper): King's Norton Station circa 1934, with one of the 1912 4-4-2 tanks built for the London Tilbury & Southend Railway. These engines were displaced from the Southend service with the coming of the Stanier 3 cylinder 2-6-4 tanks. No. 2107 is seen carrying a 21B (Bournville) shed plate, and is at the head of a Redditch train. Note the carefully stacked coal in the bunker, and the Westinghouse pump for use on the air-braked trains on the LT&SR section. The engines were stand-ins after the MR 0-6-4 tanks had finally disgraced themselves and prior to the introduction of the Stanier 2-6-2 tanks.
W. Leslie Good
P. B. Whitehouse Collection

Plate 128 (left lower): Midland Class 3P 4-4-0, No. 707, with a York to Bristol express, approaches Northfield Station around 1930. The seventh vehicle of the nine coach train has a roof destination board.
W. Leslie Good
P. B. Whitehouse Collection

Plates 131, (right upper) 132, (right lower) 133 & 134: Over the weekend of January 26th to 28th 1929, Cofton Tunnel, near Halesowen Junction on the Midland's Birmingham to Bristol main line, was demolished, and replaced by reinforced concrete supported cutting sides. These four photographs show the civil engineering work in progress. The contractors' 0-6-0 saddle tank No. 5 is Manning Wardle, No. 1793. This was part of a quadrupling scheme, from Northfield to Barnt Green.

W. Leslie Good
P. B. Whitehouse Collection

Plate 135: A scene tak[en] between 1927/8, showing [the] widening in progress betwe[en] Halesowen Junction and Ba[rnt] Green. The train, headed [by] Midland Class 2 4-4-0, No. 5[ ] is a 'down' express, and [the] engine is still in red livery.

W. Leslie Go[od]
P. B. Whitehouse Collect[ion]

Plate 136: In early LM[S] livery, Midland Class 2P 4-4[-0] No. 426 is pictured on [the] newly-quadrupled section ne[ar] Halesowen Junction at Lo[ng]bridge around 1929.

P. B. Whitehouse Collect[ion]

Plate 137: An express approaches Halesowen Junction bound for Bristol, behind one of the newer 4-4-0 Compound engines, No. 933. The wide-windowed LMS stock and upper quadrant signals place the picture in the late 1930s.

P. B. Whitehouse Collection

Plate 138: A through freight train approaches Barnt Green Station, during the spring of 1936. The engine is a Midland-built 4F class 0-6-0. Note the four tracks now extending to King's Norton, and the upper quadrant signals.

P. B. Whitehouse

Plate 139: A westbound freight train, headed by one of the LMS-built Fowler Class 4F 0-6-0s of 1927, carrying shed plate 2 (Burton). It is moving slowly towards Blackwell and the Lickey Incline, around 1928. Barnt Green Station is on the far side of the overbridge in the background, and Linthurst 'down' distant signal can be seen beside the 10th wagon.

W. Leslie Good
P. B. Whitehouse Collection

Plate 140: Ex-Midland Railway Class 3 4-4-0 No. 777 approaches Blackwell Station, with a 'down' Gloucester and Bristol fast train, circa 1929. The crossover, between the first and second coaches, is to enable the bankers, which will have dropped off whilst running through the station, to return to Bromsgrove.

W. Leslie Good
P. B. Whitehouse Collection

Plate 141: A double-headed express seen near Lickey End, towards the summit of the Lickey Incline. The nine coach train appears to have the big banker on its rear, the pilot being Johnson single, No. 679 from No. 8 shed (Bristol), and the train engine an unknown Class 2 4-4-0.

W. Leslie Good
P. B. Whitehouse Collection

Plate 142:   Ex-Midland Railway Class 3 4-4-0, No. 712, almost certainly painted red, and carrying the LMS crest on her cabside, heads a nine coach train near Blackwell, sometime during the mid-1920s. The engine carries No. 3 shed code (Saltley), and the fireman appears to be taking it easy, probably protecting his fire and letting the bankers do the work, a common practice to the end of the steam era.   *P. B. Whitehouse Collection*

Plate 143:   A Bristol to Birmingham express climbs the Lickey Incline in the early days of the LMS, probably before 1925. The engine is a No. 8 shed (Bristol) based Class 2P 4-4-0, No. 515, and the train has a single banker, indicating that it is almost certainly the great 0-10-0, No. 2290. The leading van is an oddity, this being a MR motor car van, built to Metropolitan loading gauge, and the train is of Midland stock, the engine still carrying its bogie wheel protective splashers.   *W. Leslie Good*
P. B. Whitehouse Collection

Plate 144: Still with its Salter safety valves, but lettered LMS, ex-Midland 2-4-0, No. 168 brings a train of horse-boxes up the Lickey Incline, in the mid-1920s. This time, the train engine appears to be doing its share of the work, there being only one banker, an 0-6-0 tank.

W. Leslie Good
P. B. Whitehouse Collection

Plate 145: About two-thirds of the way up the hill, two LMS-painted ex-Midland engines, in the form of an inside-framed 2-4-0, No. 158, and Class 2P 4-4-0, No. 520, head a heavy train from the south-west. There appears to be four engines with the train, as the photograph shows twin plumes of steam to the rear of the coaching stock not altogether surprising with thirteen coaches. The leading vehicle is clearly lettered 'LMS saloon'.

W. Leslie Good
P. B. Whitehouse Collection

Plate 146: The Lickey banker, as LMS No. 2290, during the last summer of the Company's existence. Nationalization was to bring considerable changes to Bromsgrove Shed, as new minds began looking at the everpresent problem of this two mile gradient of 1 in 37·7. First came the LNER Garratt, which was heartily disliked, and was dealt with accordingly. Also, when the Western Region took over the line as far as Burnt Green, a 52XX class 2-8-0 tank was used. Later, Hawkesworth 0-6-0 tanks took over the job from the LMS 'Jinty' locomotives, and served to the end of steam. In the photograph, the train enginemen have decided to take it easy and let the banker do the work.

P. B. Whitehouse

Plate 147: A Birmingham-bound freight train attacks the Lickey Incline, just out of Bromsgrove Station, with Kirtley double-framed 0-6-0, No. 2469 in charge, during early LMS days.

W. Leslie Good
P. B. Whitehouse Collection

Plate 148: The south-west end of Bromsgrove Station, with a freight train eminating from the Great Western just starting up the Lickey Incline, banked by two 'Jinty' locomotives and an ex-Midland Class 3F 0-6-0.

H. C. Casserley

Plate 149: Worcester Station in 1935, with a new LMS-built Compound, No. 935, with a Bristol to Birmingham train.

P. Hopkins

Plate 150: Although carrying the number 700, this LMS 4-4-0 is a Class 2P, its predecessor, a Midland Class 3P, having been withdrawn before its construction. No. 700 was the last of the LMS-built Class 2Ps, and was ex-works in 1932. It is shown with a 'down' local train at Gloucester, circa 1933.

P. M. Alexander

Plate 151: Malvern Station, date unknown, with a local train for Ashchurch in the LMS bay. Although Tewkesbury Shed housed an 0-6-0 the trains were usually headed by ex-Midland 0-4-4 tanks, though towards the end of steam days, Stanier 0-4-4 tanks were used on this duty. Class 3F, No. 3373 was probably filling in on a washout day.

N. E. Stead

Plates 152 & 153 (overleaf upper): Two photographs of Tewkesbury Shed on the eve of Nationalization, both showing ex-Midland engines. This small depot housed the locomotives for the Ashchurch to Malvern branch via Upton on Severn, the passenger service being worked by Midland 0-4-4 tanks, as illustrated by No. 1406. Both engines carry shed plate No. 22B (Gloucester).

P. B. Whitehouse

Plate 154: Midland Railway Class 1F open cab 0-6-0 tank, with the branch train at Dursley on 5th July 1947.

H. C. Casserley

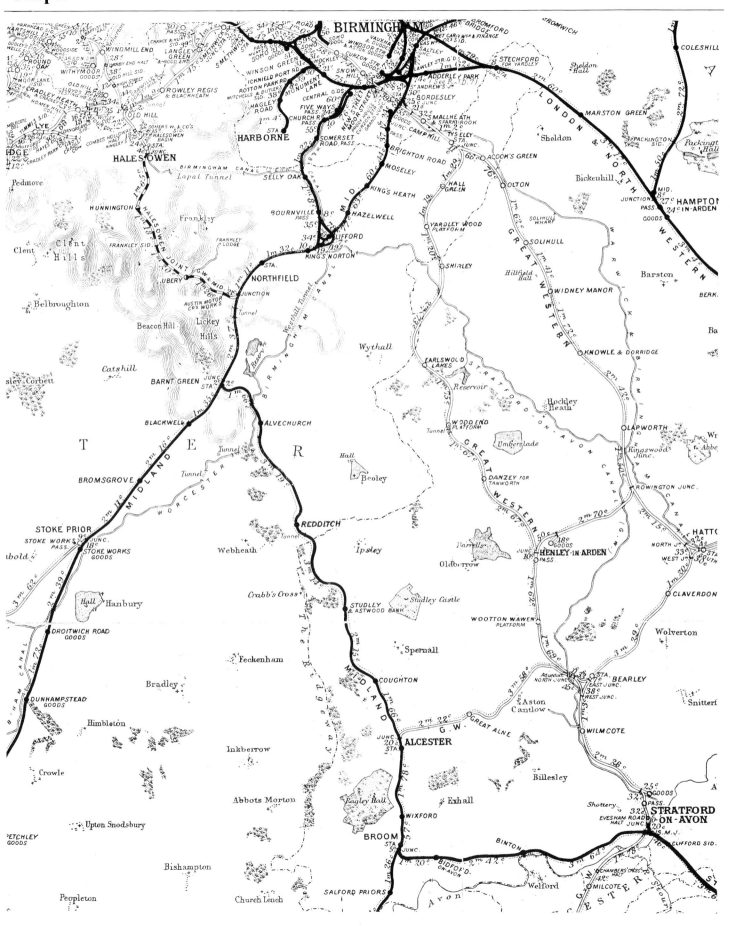

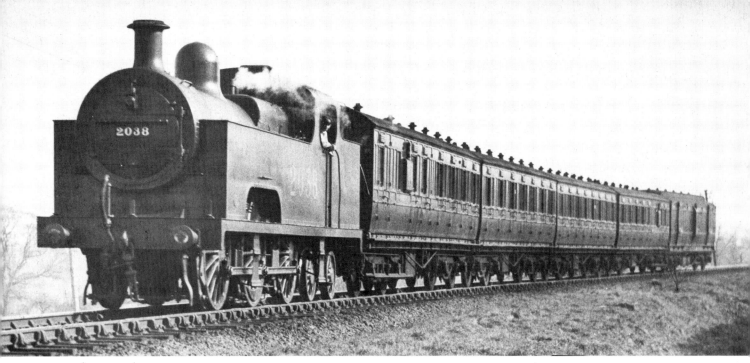

Plate 155: A Birmingham-bound Redditch branch train, seen on the single line near Barnt Green, behind ex-MR 0-6-4 tank, No. 2038. The train is made up of Midland elliptical roof suburban stock with a clerestory full brake. The picture was probably taken just after Grouping. *W. Leslie Good*
P. B. Whitehouse Collection

Plate 156: Fowler 2-6-4 tank, No. 2326 with a through Ashchurch to New Street train, running via Evesham and Redditch, and standing at Alvechurch Station.
P. B. Whitehouse

Plate 157: An ex-MR 0-6-4 tank, No. 2027 with a Birmingham (New Street) to Redditch and Ashchurch train, photographed at Broom Junction in the summer of 1933.
P. Hopkins

Plate 158: Broom Junction for Stratford-upon-Avon, pictured in the late 1930s, and looking towards Redditch. The then new upper quadrant signals control both the line to Redditch, and the goods only Stratford and Midland Junction branch.

P. B. Whitehouse

SMJ Section

STRATFORD-UPON-AVON & MIDLAND JUNCTION RAILWAY.

BEWARE OF TRAINS.

TRESPASSERS WILL BE PROSECUTED

BY ORDER.

Plate 159: A cast-iron 'beware of trains' notice on the Stratford-upon-Avon & Midland Junction Railway.

P. B. Whitehouse Collection

Plate 160: One of the small companies acquired by the LMS at the 1923 Grouping was the Stratford-upon-Avon & Midland Junction Railway. This joined Stratford, on the GWR, with the Midland & Great Central (Broom Junction, Ravenstonewood Junction and Woodford and the LNWR at Blisworth and Cockley Brake Junction). The SMJ had its own shed at Stratford, and here is SMJ No. 18, of 1908 as LMS No. 2311, on the turntable. The class of eleven engines were built by Beyer Peacock, from 1880 onwards. No. 18 was the last to be constructed, and the class was extinct by 1930.

W. Leslie Good

Plate 161: Only just in her new LMS livery, and numbered 2300, SMJ 0-6-0 No. 2 changes crews outside Stratford Old Town Station in 1924. This was one of the earlier Beyer Peacock engines, dating from 1880.

W. Leslie Good
P. B. Whitehouse Collection

Plate 162: LMS No. 2303, originally SMJ No. 7, was one of Stroudley's 0-6-0 locomotives built for the London Brighton & South Coast Railway. When made redundant there, she was sold to the SMJ in 1920, and being completely nonstandard, was scrapped by the LMS a few months after this photograph was taken in 1924.

W. Leslie Good
P. B. Whitehouse Collection

Plate 163: SMJ 0-6-0 No. 16 leaves the LMS station with a train for Towcester, around 1924. A sister engine is signalled off the shed road.

W. Leslie Good
P. B. Whitehouse Collection

Plate 164: Stratford-on-Avon-based SMJ No. 16, later LMS No. 2309, outside the shed just after Grouping probably around 1924. This was one of the last batch of heavier engines built in 1908 by Beyer Peacock.

W. Leslie Good
P. B. Whitehouse Collection

Chapter Ten – HALESOWEN BRANCH

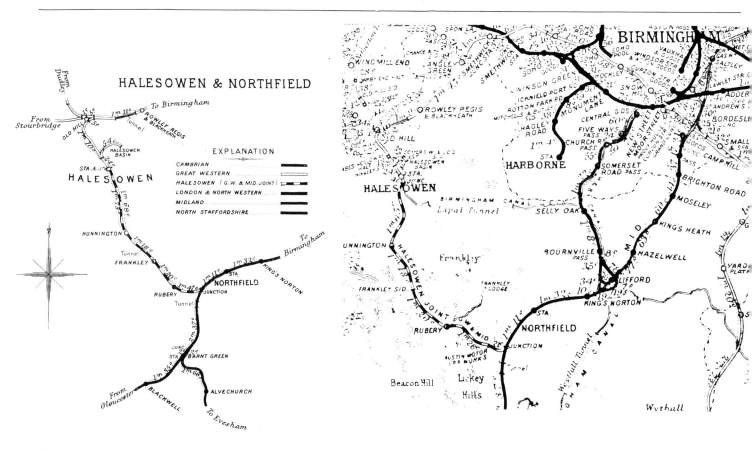

HALESOWEN & NORTHFIELD

EXPLANATION

CAMBRIAN
GREAT WESTERN
HALESOWEN (G.W. & MID. JOINT)
LONDON & NORTH WESTERN
MIDLAND
NORTH STAFFORDSHIRE

Plate 165: The Kirtley double-framed 0-6-0s of the Midland Railway were a numerous class, comprising some 470 engines. Dating from 1863, many were rebuilt by Johnson and Deeley with several variations of boiler, smokebox and cab. A few survived their less fortunate counterparts for many years at Bournville Shed, Birmingham, being specially kept to work the Halesowen branch, whose spindly Dowery Dell Viaduct required severe weight restrictions. They were finally replaced in 1951 by the slightly larger Class 2F 0-6-0s. No. 22834 was photographed on Bournville Shed in 1935.

R. G. Jarvis
Colourviews Picture Library

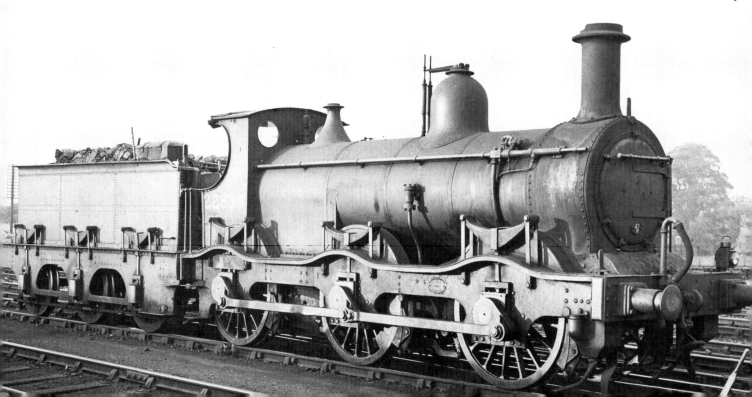

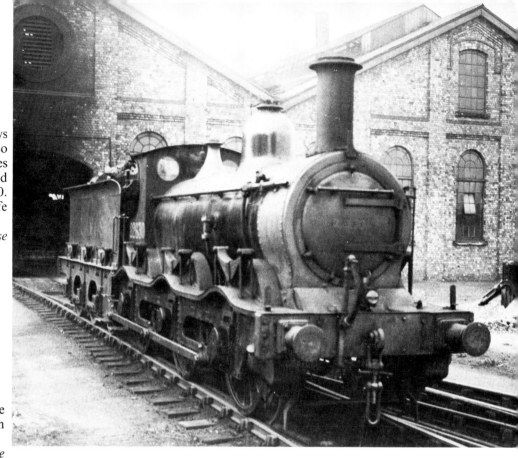

Plate 166: By 1938, Stanier chimneys were *de rigeur*, and No. 22630 had been so fitted. This was one of the four engines to survive into British Railways days, and the only one to carry a BR number – 58110. It was scrapped in 1951, after a working life of 81 years.

P. B. Whitehouse

Plate 167: Rubery Station which was the first stop and only passing loop between Longbridge and Halesowen.

P. B. Whitehouse

Plate 168: Rubery Station, just after Nationalization with a MR Johnson Class 2F 0-6-0 picking up the staff with an afternoon goods train bound for Halesowen.

P. B. Whitehouse

Plate 169: An ex-Midland Railway Class 2F 0-6-0 climbs up from Dowery Dell towards Rubery, with a Halesowen to Halesowen Junction freight train, in the summer of 1947. These engines were just beginning to take over from the Kirtley double-framed 0-6-0 locomotives.

P. B. Whitehouse

Plate 170: An unknown Midland Kirtley double-framed 0-6-0 climbs up from Halesowen and Dowery Dell to Frankley Beeches, during the late autumn of 1935. The cast-iron notice, below the locomotive's tender, proclaims ownership by the Great Western & Midland Railways, and warns trespassers of possible fines of up to forty shillings.

F. E. Hemming

Plate 171: Another Kirtley 0-6-0 outside-framed locomotive, No. 22852, returning from Halesowen towards Hunnington with a train of empty car vans, in May 1935.

H. C. Casserley

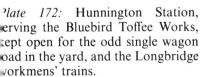

Plate 172: Hunnington Station, serving the Bluebird Toffee Works, kept open for the odd single wagon load in the yard, and the Longbridge workmens' trains.

P. B. Whitehouse

Chapter Eleven – RUGBY

Plate 173: Carrying shed plate No. 8 (Rugby), newly-delivered 'Royal Scot' class 4-6-0, No. 6115 stands alongside the protective glass windscreen at the side of Rugby station, on 5th November 1927. At the time of the photograph, it has yet to be named, and is carrying early livery with tender numerals and the company's crest on the cabside. It was later named *Scots Guardsman*, and has since been preserved.

A. W. Flowers

Plate 174: An Upperby 'Royal Scot' class 4-6-0, No. 6137 *The Prince of Wales's Volunteers South Lancashire* takes the slack through Rugby and heads for home with the 10.05 Euston to Perth service. The picture dates from 1936, deduced from the block figures, vacuum pump, and angled smoke deflectors.

P. B. Whitehouse Collection

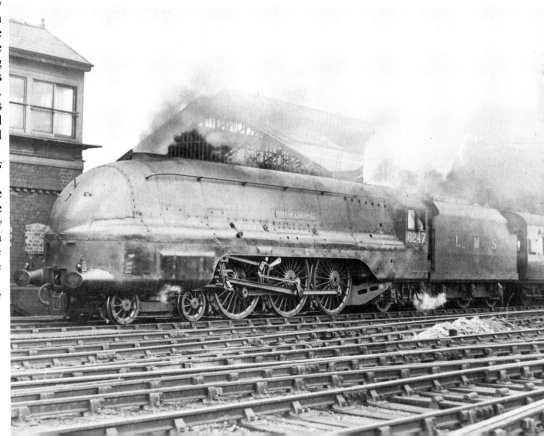

Plate 175: A somewhat grimy *Duchess of Gloucester* passes through Rugby during 1938, at the head of the first part of the 'Royal Scot' made up to fifteen coaches. The reporting number W63/1 indicates that this was the 09.55 Euston to Glasgow service. At that time, No. 6225 was painted in red and gold, and the coal streaks on her casing were unusual for a streamliner.

A. W. Flowers

Plate 176: In sombre wartime black, but still streamlined, one of the later Stanier Pacifics, No. 6247 *City of Liverpool* waits at Rugby, with a 'down' express in 1945. Note the glass, which is still in place on the right-hand roof gable.

A. W. Flowers

Plate 177: On her usual Liverpool duty, Stanier's Turbomotive Pacific halts at Rugby on her way north, in January 1948, just after Nationalization.

A. W. Flowers

Plate 178: The south end of Rugby Station, pictured in 1947. The Webb 2-4-2 tank has gold blocked lettering, later type lamp brackets, and Ross pop safety-valves, and is heading 1930s LMS suburban stock. The train is in the Northampton bay, probably destined for Peterborough.

A. W. Flowers

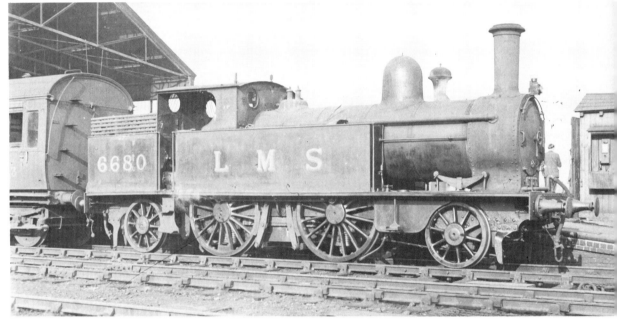

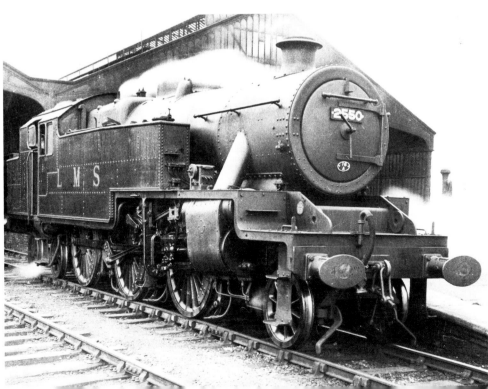

Plate 179 A new Stanier two cylinder 2-6-4 tank, No. 2550 from No. 16A shed (Nottingham), in the Midland bay at Rugby during 1936. This will have worked through with one of the all stations trains, running via the Leicester branch.

A. W. Flowers

Plate 180: One of Rugby's 2-4-0 LNWR 'Precedent' class locomotives, taken from the south end of the station platform, circa 1930. The engine is No. 5011 *Director*, which was then in regular use on the branch to Leamington and Warwick.

W. Leslie Good
P. B. Whitehouse Collection

Plates 181, 182 & 183: Three 'Claughton' class locomotives on the depot in 1933, all of them from LNWR shed No. 1 (Camden), finished in lined out LMS red. The engines are No 5939 *Clio*, and unnamed Nos. 5989 and 5980. The latter two are carrying excursion headboards, and are coaled up ready for the return journey. The engines were very much in the twilight of their days, as the building of the 'Jubilee' class 4-6-0 locomotives and the Stanier 'Black Fives' from 1934, ensured the total demise of those unrebuilt by 1935.

W. Leslie Good
P. B. Whitehouse Collection

Plates 185, 186 & 187: Locomotives from three Chief Mechanical Engineers, George Whale, George Hughes and Henry Fowler, in the turntable area close to the Great Central overbridge, in 1933. The 'Experiment' class 4-6-0, No. 5535 *Cheshire* was nearing the end of her days, and would have been used on the Euston semi-fast trains. The other two locomotives were her partial successors, at least until the Stanier era, which was not far off.

W. Leslie Good
P. B. Whitehouse Collection

Plate 184 (opposite): Rugby Shed in March 1933, featuring ex-Midland Class 2F 0-6-0, No. 2912.

P. B. Whitehouse Collection

Plate 188: At the time, Rugby also housed this Fowler 0-8-0, No. 9674, with feed water heaters, shed plate No. 8, and no vacuum gear on the front. The date is 1933; the class was not introduced until 1929, and this was the last locomotive to be built and the last 0-8-0 to be constructed in Great Britain.

W. Leslie Good
P. B. Whitehsouse Collection

Plate 189: A Northampton-Blisworth-Leamington-Warwick train at Blisworth, on 19th April 1947. The engine, a 2-4-2 LNWR Webb 5ft. 6in. radial tank from Northampton, is pushing its train across from the 'up' fast to the 'down' fast line, prior to making its way down the main line to Weedon. From here, it will branch off to Leamington, via Daventry.

W. A. Camwell

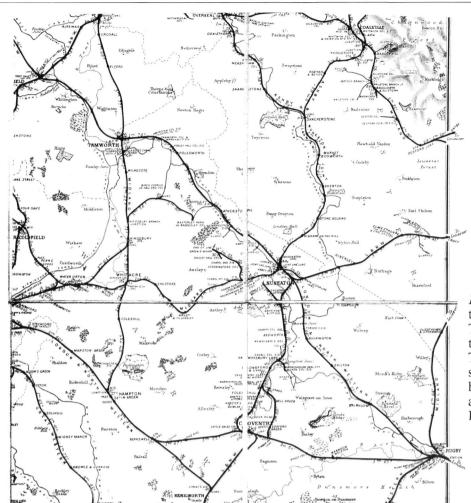

Rugby – Nuneaton – Tamworth

Plate 190: An 'up' fast train on Newbold troughs, just north of Rugby, circa 1928. The engine is in LMS red with the crest on the cabside, and is trailing a black tender. The cast-iron smokebox numberplate 5274 shows that the locomotive is the super-heated 'Precursor' class *Hecate*, a very appropriate name considering the shriek of LNWR whistles.

A. W. Flowers

Plate 191: A 'down' express train, double-headed by 'George the Fifth' class 4-4-0, No. 5350 *India* and 'Prince of Wales' class 4-6-0, No. 5634 *William Cowper*. The former was soon to have her nameplate stripped, after the construction of the 'Jubilee' class locomotive of the same name. *India* was the last pure 'George the Fifth' class locomotive to remain in service. The date is circa 1928, and the location is Kingbury, near Newbold.

A. W. Flowers

Plate 192 (below): A double-headed 'down' train of empty stock is pictured near Newbold in 1928. Both the Hughes 'Crab' locomotives are unknown, but carry numbers in the 13XXX series on their tenders.

A. W. Flowers

Plate 193: The 'down' 'Coronation Scot', passing Shilton in 1937. The whole train is finished in blue and silver, and the engine is a brand-new Pacific, No. 6223 *Princess Alice*.

A. W. Flowers

Plate 194: Pictured during 1928, an 'up' express passes Shilton, approximately half-way between Nuneaton and Rugby, hauled by re-boilered 'Claughton' class 4-6-0, No. 5927 *Sir Francis Dent*. The train is fourteen coaches long, and includes three Midland clerestory vehicles and an LNWR six wheel bogie diner.

A. W. Flowers

Plate 195: A 'down' local train, running from Rugby to Stafford, headed by 'Prince of Wales' class 4-6-0, No. 5662 *Anzac*, seen at Shilton in 1928.

A. W. Flowers

Plate 196: A 'down' main line express north of Rugby, circa 1928, headed by LNWR Webb-designed 'Precedent' class 2-4-0, No. 5062 *Sir Alexander Cockburn*, and 'Claughton' class 4-6-0, No. 5967 *L/Cpl J. A. Christie, V.C.*

A. W. Flowers

Plate 197: About 200 yds. short of Bulkington Station, a George Whale 19in. goods 4-6-0, No. 8736 takes a partially-fitted fast freight train northwards towards Nuneaton. The photograph was taken in 1928.

A. W. Flowers

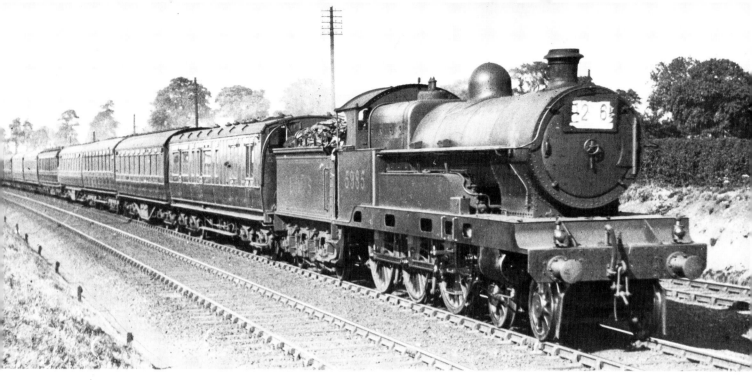

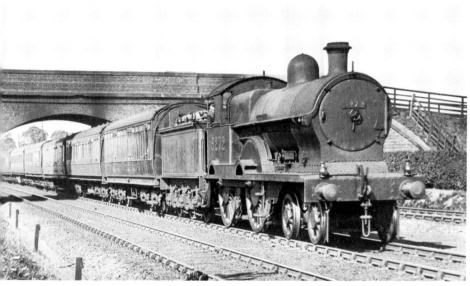

Plate 198 (above): An unnamed 'Claughton' class 4-6-0, No. 5985, with an 'up' fast train near Bulkington, south of Nuneaton, in 1928. The last six coaches carry roof boards, and the fifth from the locomotive is an LNWR six-wheel bogie diner, indicating a train of some importance.

A. W. Flowers

Plate 199: Superheated 'Precursor' class 4-4-0, No. 5272 *Brindley* heads an 'up' fast train near Nuneaton, during 1928.

A. W. Flowers

Plate 200: A No. 4 shed (Nuneaton) based 'Experiment' class 4-6-0, No. 5525 *Byzantium* heads an 'up' semi-fast train in 1930. The scene is between Nuneaton and Bulkington.

A. W. Flowers

Plate 201: LNWR Bowen-Cooke 0-8-2 tank No. 7878, shunts at Nuneaton (Trent Valley goods yard during 1927.

A. W. Flower.

Plate 202: London & North Western, Lancashire & Yorkshire, Midland Chief Mechanical Engineers have locomotives side by side, at Nuneaton Shed in the mid-1920s. Hughes 2-6-0, No. 13032 was almost new at the time, and very much dwarfs the small Webb 0-6-2 coal tank, whilst sitting under the LNWR combined coal stage and water tank. The tender of a Midland Class 3F 0-6-0 protrudes into the right of the photograph.

P. B. Whitehouse Collection

Plate 203: 'Prince of Wales' class 4-6-0, No. 5635 Charles Lamb, finished in crimson lake, takes a train of fitted stock over the crossover from the slow line approaching Nuneaton (Trent Valley) Station, in 1927. The coaching stock appears to be freshly painted, and it is a reasonable surmise that most of this was done at Wolverton. The train is made up to twenty vehicles. On the left is one of the few remaining 'Renown' class locomotives, which were all were gone by 1931. It was possibly LNWR No. 1901 Jubilee.

A. W. Flowers

Plate 204: Still carrying its LNWR number, but painted plain black, Webb's onetime four cylinder Compound, No. 1901 *Jubilee* is shown rebuilt, by Whale, as a two cylinder Simple. It is shown standing at Nuneaton Shed in 1926. As rebuilt the class was known after the name of the first reconstructed engine *Renown*.

A. W. Flowers

Plate 205: An evening picture, taken just after 7.25 p.m., showing Webb's 18in. goods 0-6-0, No. 1775 at Nuneaton (Trent Valley) platform 1, in 1925. It is at the head of a Leamington via Coventry local train, and the stock is still carrying LNWR livery. Note the old type headlamp sockets, which were in use prior to lamp brackets.

A. W. Flowers

Plate 206: A 'down' Liverpool express train, behind 'Royal Scot' class 4-6-0, No. 6143, fitted with new smoke deflectors, and carrying shed plate No. 26 (Edge Hill). The tender is of Fowler straight-sided design. A sign of the times is the passenger leaning out of the window for the paperboy, who is running down the platform. The LNWR water-column is complete with brazier, against winter climes.

A. W. Flowers

Plate 207: A 'down' loca
train to Stafford passes Ashb
Junction, just north of Nur
eaton (Trent Valley) Statio
double-headed by Fowler Clas
4F 0-6-0, No. 4389, and a
unknown 'Prince of Wale:
class 4-6-0. The year is 1930.
A. W. Flower

Plate 208: An Easter 193
photograph of ex-Midlan
0-4-4 tank, No. 1369 leavin
Nuneaton (Trent Valley), an
about to cross over to th
Ashby and Burton line, close
to all regular passenger trains i
April 1931.

A. W. Flower

Plate 209: 'Royal Scot' class 4-6-0, No. 6139 *The Welch Regiment*, seen near Tamworth around 1930. This is the 'up' 9.00 a.m. Glasgow to Euston 'Royal Scot', thirteen coaches long, and with a newly-built full bogie brake, attached to the small Fowler flat-sided tender.

W. Leslie Good

Plate 210: An unnamed LNWR 'Claughton' class 4-6-0, possibly No. 6006, double-heads a smoke deflectored 'Royal Scot' class locomotive with a straight-sided tender, on a 'down' express south of Tamworth, around 1933/4. The train is heavy in weight, comprising sixteen vehicles, and of particular note is the leading steel-sided coach, brand-new at the time.

W. Leslie Good

Plate 211: 'George the Fifth' class 4-4-0, No. 1417 *Landrail* (later re-numbered LMS No. 5370), photographed from the footbridge just south of Tamworth Station, sometime in the mid-1920s. The leading Midland cleres-tory coach has had its panels over-painted and lettered LMS, whilst the second coach is entirely repainted in the new livery. The four coach set, at the rear of the bogie full brake, is still in LNWR colours as is *Landrail*, which has its tender fully lined out.

P. B. Whitehouse Collection

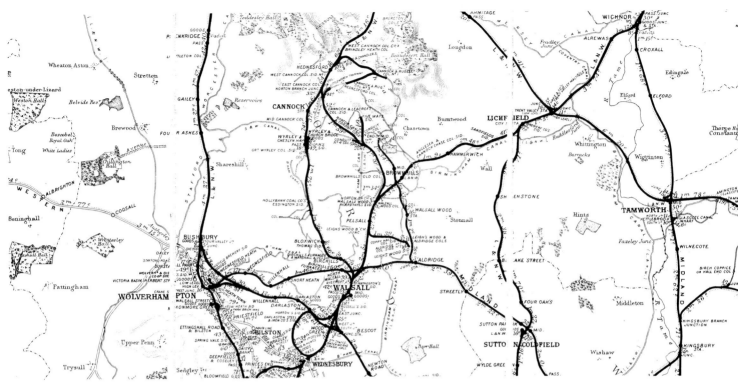

Plate 212: Atherstone Station, between Nuneaton and Tamworth, photographed on 6th May 1946. The signal box, perched high above the footbridge, gave excellent views of all traffic, including the working of the goods yard. Atherstone lies in the centre of the Warwickshire Coalfield.

H. C. Casserley

Plates 213, 214 & 215: Three photographs, showing the early days of the LMS, taken south of Tamworth on the old LNWR main line, where the fast lines were in the middle of the quadrupled tracks. These pictures show the variety of liveries on display during the early to middle 1920s. The double-headed train has 2-4-0 'Precedent' class, No. 478 *Commodore*, in its old livery, piloting a red 'Claughton' class locomotive with a cast-iron smokebox numberplate. The leading vehicle is a six-wheeled bogie diner, in LNWR plum and spilt milk. With two locomotives and six coaches, it is little wonder that there is still plenty of coal in the tenders. The 'Experiment' class 4-6-0, No. 5454 *Sarmatian* is

still in lined out LNWR livery, but carries its new LMS cast-iron smokebox numberplate whilst the coaches appear to be of a mixed variety, the first two being in the old colours and the last vehicle in LMS livery. The third photograph shows an unknown 'Renown' class rebuilt 4-4-0 Compound, possibly No. 5135 *Euryalus*. This still has headlamp sockets, but is in the new LMS livery, with large Midland style numerals on the tender. At least three of the six coaches are in LNWR livery.

W. Leslie Good
P. B. Whitehouse Collection

Plate 216: Another picture, taken south of Tamworth, showing 'Claughton' class 4-6-0, No. 5908 *Alfred Fletcher* on test. The engine, one of ten such locomotives, has just been fitted with Caprotti valve gear, in an attempt to obtain improved performance. Along with nineteen other members of the class, No. 5908 was later fitted with a larger boiler.
P. B. Whitehouse Collection

Plate 217: Smart and clean in its old LNWR livery, 'Precedent' class 2-4-0, No. 2194 *Cambrian* waits at Tamworth, complete with class A headlamps but with non-corridor stock. The year is 1924, when the new red coaches were in the minority, and a LNW liveried train was not a rare sight. It was, however, unusual to see an old lady like this in such pristine condition, with cab spectacle plates polished and paintwork really gleaming. Perhaps it was a determination somewhere that the Midland takeover was not quite an accomplished fact.

Roger Carpenter Collection

Plate 218 (below): Unnamed ex-LNWR 'Prince of Wales' class 4-6-0, No. 25752 leaves Tamworth, with a Rugby to Stafford local train, just into Nationalization.
E. S. Russell

Plate 219: Re-boilered 'Royal Scot' class 4-6-0, No. 6160 *Queen Victoria's Rifleman* passes Tamworth, with a Euston to Manchester express. The spur up to the Midland line can be seen to the left of the locomotive.

E. S. Russell

Plate 220: Ex-LNWR 0-8-0, No. 9264 is pictured shunting a mineral train at Tamworth. The train has arrived from the Rugby direction, probably from Baddesley Colliery near Atherstone. Having run through the station, it has reversed, crossed from 'down' fast to 'up' fast line, and is in the process of crossing from the 'up' fast, on which the locomotive is travelling, to the 'up' slow or platform road. Once clear of the crossover, it will draw forward and reverse again up the spur to the Midland Derby to Bristol line, which can be seen crossing the LNWR main line in the background. The ultimate destination is either Hams Hall Power-Station or Coleshill or Washwood Heath Yard in Birmingham.

E. S. Russell

Plate 221: A 'down' express train, hauled by a Hughes L&Y type 4-6-0, takes water on Hademore troughs in the mid-1920s. After the initial enthusiasm for these engines, West Coast expresses reverted to one-time LNWR engines, until the coming of the 'Royal Scot' class locomotives in 1927. The coaching stock is, in the main, still in North Western livery.

P. B. Whitehouse Collection

Plate 222: A northbound express train, headed by an unknown Hughes 4-6-0, and piloted by 'Prince of Wales' class 4-6-0, No. 5647 *Edith Cavell,* passes over Hademore troughs near Lichfield in the 1920s.

A. W. Flowers

Plate 223: An unknown LNWR 'Super D' class 0-8-0 takes a perishable and vacuum-fitted class C freight train over Hademore troughs towards Lichfield (Trent Valley) just after Nationalization. Note that, even at this late date the locomotive still retains its old LNWR chimney.

E. S. Russell

Plate 224 (above): Guardians of Lichfield Station, photographed in 1939.In reality, they are the upper quadrant bracket signals, at the south end of the station.

P. B. Whitehouse

Plate 225 (left): The 'down' 'Coronation Scot' approaches Lichfield, a week after the service started in July 1937. The engine is No. 6222 *Queen Mary* and, like its train, is finished in blue and silver livery.

F. E. Hemming

Plates 226, 227 & 228: Lichfield, in 1939, as seen from the overbridge to the south of the station. Looking north is the dual Trent Valley station, with its main line tracks bifurcating to provide platform and through roads for stoppers and expresses respectively. It is crossed at high level by the wooden station carrying the branch from Lichfield (City) to Burton and Wichnor Junction, where it meets the Midland Railway. (Note the spotters bicycles on the footpath!) The 'up' trains are headed by the then new streamlined Pacifics in red and gold including No. 6229 *Duchess of Hamilton*, and 'Patriot' class 4-6-0, No. 5545. The 'down' train is behind 'Royal Scot' class, No. 6142 *The York & Lancaster Regiment*.

P. B. Whitehouse

Plate 229: An 'up' express, leaving Lichfield (Trent Valley), around 1930. Note, in the background, the high level branch to Burton. The engine is 'Royal Scot' class 4-6-0, No. 6137 *Vesta*, named after an earlier locomotive, but it was later renamed *The Prince of Wales's Volunteers South Lancashire*. The train is probably the 'up' 'Royal Scot'.

F. E. Hemming

Plate 230 (below): Lichfield (Trent Valley) Station in 1937, looking south from the 'down' platform, with an unknown 'Royal Scot' class locomotive heading a 'down' excursion on the through track.

C. C. Hoare

Plate 231: Looking north from Lichfield (Trent Valley), during the snowy winter of 1939/40. The steam-wreathed engine on the right is an ex-LNWR 'Super D' 0-8-0, with an 'up' freight train.

P. B. Whitehouse

Plate 232: The original station buildings at Lichfield (Trent Valley), built by the Trent Valley Railway, although opened in 1847 after this and two other companies combined in 1846 to become the LNWR. They are situated on the 'down' side of the line, to the north of the present station. The combined style of Victorian and Elizabethan architecture can also be seen at Colwich, Polesworth and Atherstone, and traces still remain at Tamworth. Note also, the row of standard LNWR employees' cottages, to the left of the photograph.   *E. S. Russell*

Plate 233: 'Down' Nuneaton to Stafford local train, on the main line north of Lichfield, taken in the late 1920s. The locomotive is a red painted and lined out ex-LNWR 'Prince of Wales' class 4-6-0, No. 5675 *Sphinx.* It is the nearest that one-time North Western engines ever came to being 'Midlandized', with regards to colour, smokebox plates, crest on cabside and numerals on tenders.

P. B. Whitehouse Collection

Plate 234: Rugeley (Trent Valley) No. 1 'down' home signal gantry, frames 'Royal Scot' class 4-6-0, No. 6142 *The York & Lancaster Regiment*, on the 'up' Welshman. Apart from the removal of the rings from the slow line signals, these splendid 'skyscrapers' remained as installed by the LNWR well into BR days. All other Trent Valley line signals, controlled by No. 1 box, remained original North Western until electrification. However, signals controlled by Rugeley No. 2 box, at the north end of the station, were replaced pre-war by the LMS standard upper quadrant signals on tubular posts. The branch from Walsall is seen coming in to the left of the picture.

E. S. Russell

Plate 235: One of the few LNWR 'Experiment' class 4-6-0 locomotives to be renumbered in the 20,000s during the 1934 scheme was No. 5552 *Denbighshire*, shown here with an 'up' Dudley half-day excursion, circa 1932. The first six coaches are all North Stafford and are painted in LMS livery, as is the locomotive. The use of these close-coupled six wheeled sets for Saturday excursions was far from unusual, and this train has twelve of them, plus two six wheeled full brake vans. Both distant signals are on, and the engine is shut off in readiness for the junction. The train is between Colwich and Rugeley.

W. Leslie Good

Plate 236: The 10.35 Euston to Manchester fast train, double-headed by a Midland Compound 4-4-0 and a LNWR 'Claughton' class 4-6-0, near Rugeley circa 1932.

W. Leslie Good

Plate 237: A 'down' express seen near Rugeley in August 1934, headed by a then unnamed 'Jubilee' class 4-6-0, No. 5608, and 'Royal Scot' class 4-6-0, No. 6127 *The Old Contemptibles*. Both engines carry straight sided 3,500 gallon Fowler tenders.

W. Leslie Good

Plate 238: An unknown LNWR 19in. goods 4-6-0 locomotive, working hard but steaming well, seen taking an 'up' slow goods train out of the southern portal of Shugborough Tunnel, sometime during the early 1930s. This was the plain uncastellated southern portal, the northern end being so decorated to fit in with early landowners' requirements.

W. Leslie Good

Stafford – Crewe

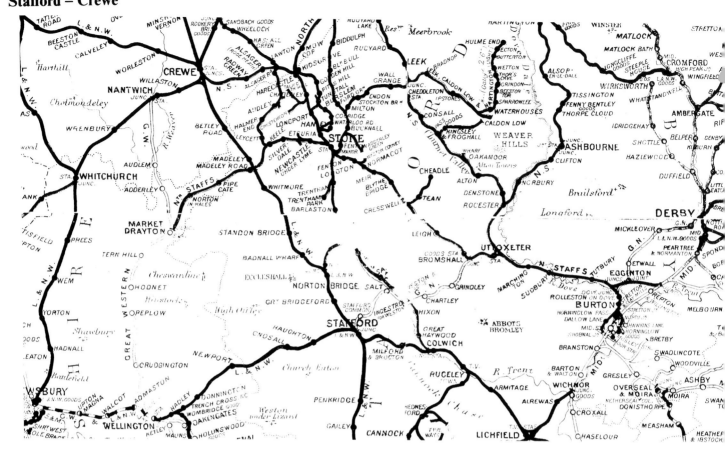

Plates 239 & 240 Taking water at Whitmore on the four tracked troughs circa 1932/3. The 'down' express on the fast line is the 11.50 a.m. service from Euston to Manchester and Liverpool, headed by a re-boilered 'Claughton' class No. 5946 *Duke of Connaught*, resplendent in red. The local 'up' train is a Crewe bound ex-Stafford set behind an unnamed, black 'Prince of Wales' locomotive, No. 5825.

W. Leslie Good

Plate 241: An 'up' train on Whitmore troughs circa 1932/3 the 3.05 p.m. Manchester to Birmingham express, made up to nine coaches behind unnamed 'Prince of Wales' class, No. 5831. The coal, stacked high on the tender, indicates that the engine has come on at Crewe.

W. Leslie Good

Plate 242: The 2.00 p.m. Liverpool to London express nears Gresty Lane, in the early 1930s. The engines are superheated 'Precursor' class 4-4-0, No. 5290 *Achilles* double-heading unnamed 'Claughton' class 4-6-0, No. 5988.

W. H. Whitworth

Plate 243: Sometime in the late 1920s, two LNWR express engines wait, in the traditional spot by the side of Crewe Station, to take incoming trains further to the north and west. The superheated 'Precursor' class locomotive is No. 5289 *Leviathan*, probably waiting for a Chester bound train. It is in the final form of the class, fitted with Belpaire firebox and small wheel bosses. The Jumbo is No. 5029 *Speke*, which is almost certainly bound for Carlisle as pilot to a Scotland bound train, as it carries express headlamps. Both were to suffer the axe within a few years, with the coming of the 'Royal Scot' class locomotives and the Stanier destruction of LNWR classes, Nos. 5029 and 5289 leaving operational service in 1931 and 1936 respectively.

W. H. Whitworth

Plate 244 (above): Crewe, sometime in 1927/8, featuring the then new 'Royal Scot' class 4-6-0 No. 6129 *Comet* with a 'down' express. The engine was later named *The Scottish Horse*, and is shown as originally built without smoke deflectors.

P. M. Alexander

Plate 245: An 'up' north Wales and Chester to Birmingham excursion approaches Crewe during September 1928, behind 'Renown' class 4-4-0, No. 5152 *King Arthur*, rebuilt from a Webb 4 cylinder Compound engine by George Whale. The other locomotive is 'George the Fifth' class 4-4-0, No. 5402 *Carnarvon*. The former was a No. 22 shed (Holyhead) based engine, the latter being from No. 34 shed (Patricroft).

C. J. Nevitt

Plate 246: Pictured at Crewe Station, as LNWR No. 298, is a Webb 4ft. 6in. 2-4-2 tank, in early LMS days. Note the locomotive has headlamp brackets not LNWR sockets, and the leading vehicle, a van, appears to be in red. This was the first LNWR class to be fitted for auto-working, superseding the uneconomical steam rail motor-cars, which were only powerful enough to pull themselves.

P. B. Whitehouse Collection

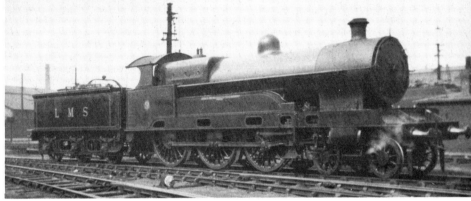

Plate 247: A common enough sight during the early days of the Grouping, with ex-LNWR 'Claughton' class 4-6-0, No. 591 *W. E. Dorrington* at Crewe North Shed. The engine is painted red and the tender in black, this basically happening during two periods, firstly when the edict went out to paint passenger engines red, and secondly, when this was partly reversed. This picture was taken in the later period, with the locomotive seen in early LMS colours.

P. M. Alexander

Plate 248: Crewe North Shed, sometime after 1935, when the new coaling stage had been installed and LNWR passenger engines were being scrapped almost daily. This unnamed 'Prince of Wales' class 4-6-0, No. 25732 carries a shed plate No. 5A, indicating that Crewe was its home. It was probably used for workings to Manchester or Stafford via Stoke, and with local trains to Shrewsbury.

P. B. Whitehouse Collection

Plate 249: The remains of LNWR 'Prince of Wales' class 4-6-0, No. 25648 *Queen of the Belgians*, are pictured at Crewe, on 7th October 1934. Her condition was the result of a derailment at Warrington, but she was later rebuilt, and was not withdrawn until 1947.

C. J. Nevitt

Plate 250: Crewe erecting shop, during the early 1930s, when LNWR engines were still carrying smokebox numberplates. On the left, having a valve rebore, is 'Super D' 0-8-0, No. 9430, whilst on the right is No. 9398 of the same class, heading two of her sisters. An 'Experiment' class 4-6-0 is sandwiched in between them. Both the existence of the numberplate and the presence of the 'Experiment' point to this date approximation.

P. B. Whitehouse Collection

Plates 251, 252 (right upper), 253 (right lower): Crewe Works, in 1936. These three photographs show an interesting selection of locomotives under repair and storage, including 'Royal Scot' class 4-6-0 No. 6125 *3rd Carabinier,* an unknown LNWR 'George the Fifth' class 4-4-0, a 2-6-0 + 0-6-2 Garratt with the later revolving bunker, and the ex-Leek & Manifold Light Railway 2-6-4 tank *J. B. Earle.* The latter was stored in the works between 1934 and 1937, being officially withdrawn on 23rd February 1935. There was talk of it being sold to the West Indies, but nothing came of it. The engine was sold to George Cohen & Sons, and scrapped in May 1937.

A. W. Flowers

Plate 254: The 'up' Irish Mail train passes Beeston Castle, Cheshire behind 'Royal Scot' class 4-6-0 No. 6118 *Royal Welch Fusilier*, during the early 1930s.

P. M. Alexander

Plate 255: 'Royal Scot' class 4-6-0, No. 6109 *Royal Engineer*, with an early arrangement of small smoke deflecting plates, and an experimental conical smokebox door, serving the same purpose.

P. M. Alexander

Plates 256: The 'Claughton' class locomotives were still hard at work on the Crewe, Chester and North Wales services in 1930, when this photograph was taken of a 'down' express passing Hartford.

P. M. Alexander

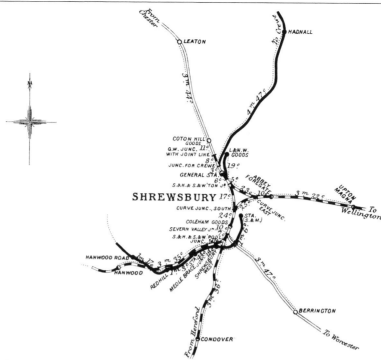

Plates 257 & 258 (overleaf top): Two photographs of Shrewsbury shed, taken on 5th March 1939, showing the old and the new together. Stanier 4-6-0 locomotives had, by now, taken a firm hold, and the main slaughter of the LNWR express passenger classes was underway. No. 25282 *Champion* is seen coaled up, waiting for a train to Crewe or Stafford, whilst the new 'Black Five' No. 5397 stands back to back with one of her sisters, and alongside an LNWR 'Super D' 0-8-0 locomotive.

P. M. Alexander

Plate 260: One of the early LNWR 'Prince of Wales' class 4-6-0 locomotives, No. 5688 *Tara*, seen with a Stafford via Wellington train at Shrewsbury in the 1920s. This was one of the engines rebuilt in 1923/4 with outside Walschaerts valve gear, nicknamed 'Tishy' after the racehorse which had a propensity to cross its legs whilst running. No. 5688 was one of the ten engines of its class never renumbered in the 20,000 series, having been withdrawn prior to their introduction in 1934. Note the glass side screening still in place on the side of the station.

C. J. Nevitt

Plate 261: Minsterley Station, on 26th August 1946, with the ancient LNWR Webb engines still in business. On the left is 0-6-0 coal engine, No. 28204, with the branch freight train, whilst on the right is 0-6-2 coal tank, No. 7740, with a passenger train to Shrewsbury, made up of GWR coaches.

W. A. Camwell

Plate 259 (opposite): An unknown 'Tishy' 'Prince of Wales' class 4-6-0 (probably No. 5688 *Tara*) brings a train of ancient GWR stock from Hereford into Shrewsbury, sometime during the 1920s.

P. B. Whitehouse Collection

Plate 262:   Whitchurch in Shropshire was the junction where the Crewe to Shrewsbury line met that coming in from Chester, and the Cambrian line from Oswestry. LNWR 'Precedent' class 2-4-0, No. 5020 *Delhi* leaves with a Chester (via Malpas) train of non-corridor stock, one afternoon in the late 1920s. The engine on the parcels train to the right of the picture is either a 'George the Fifth' class 4-4-0 or 'Experiment' class 4-6-0.

C. J. Nevitt